"*Christian Confidence* is an
and useful survey of apc
evangelism in today's woi
Michael Green, Oxford University

"Chris Sinkinson has achieved something rather remarkable here. In just
a few hundred pages he looks at the craft of apologetics from almost every
angle. He examines the history of apologetics, methodology, key figures
in the discipline and the most important arguments. And he does all this
with wit and terrific style. One of the best introductions to apologetics I
have seen."
Craig J. Hazen, Biola University

"*Christian Confidence* is a masterful introduction to the whole scope of
apologetics. Here you will find a survey of the significance and role of
apologetics from its earliest masters to its finest present exemplars. It's a
great first book for new Christians embedded in an often-hostile culture
and a reminder to mature Christians of the richness of their intellectual
and faith-bound history. We join a multitude of witnesses to Christ and
his kingdom. This book will help us to do so with gusto and love, brilliance
and humility."
James W. Sire, author of *The Universe Next Door* and *A Little Primer on
Humble Apologetics*

"Now you can experience what Moorlands College students enjoy
firsthand: a reasoned, clear, accessible introduction to defending the faith
from one of the most able younger apologists I know. Fasten your seat
belt for a whistle-stop tour from ancient Greek philosophers via
Enlightenment thinkers through to worldviews of twenty-first-century
thinkers as diverse as Alvin Plantinga and Richard Dawkins. Read and you
will discover that you have many reasons to rejoice in having 'Christian
Confidence'!"
Steve Brady, Moorlands College, Christchurch, England

"This is an astonishing book for every thinking Christian. Its scope is
enormous, but its arguments are well-researched and cogently presented.
I wish I had read it years ago!"
John Risbridger, Above Bar Church, Southampton, England

"If you feel that you should apologize for apologetics or think that it's just for the experts, then this book is for you. Chris Sinkinson's brilliant introduction to Christian apologetics will help every Christian give a reason for the hope that they have. An essential textbook for any Christian who not only wants to understand apologetics but more importantly wants to help their friends overcome barriers to belief. Chris has a brilliant ability of making the complicated simple. His lectures in apologetics at Moorlands College have been the highlight for many of the students. Now you can get the benefit without leaving your armchair."

Michael Ots, evangelist among university students in the UK and Europe

"Chris Sinkinson's new book *Christian Confidence* is a surprise gift for curious minds. It is unputdownable, packed with relevant information, little-known facts and one of the most clear and wide-ranging presentations I've ever read on the vital subject of apologetics. I predict a wide readership and significant impact on those willing to test great ideas. . . . In a world suffering from an epidemic of truth decay, one great need is for Christians to be able to defend their faith convincingly among rival perspectives that compete with or attack Christianity. This scintillating, crystal-clear introduction to all the big issues is wide-ranging, intelligent and totally accessible. Readers will rediscover solid foundations for a faith that is real, and a biblical worldview that can hold its own in any debate with those open to truth. Even the hardened skeptic will be made to think and perhaps, think again."

Greg Haslam, Westminster Chapel, London

"This volume presents a helpful overview, exhibiting several strengths while introducing the field of Christian apologetics. Initially, it surveys a wide range of essential cognate areas, from critical thinking, to methodology, to a brief survey of apologetics through the centuries. Another asset is its treatment of several specific issues of current interest, such as Darwinism, Old Testament archaeology, scientific cosmology, pluralism, and the perennial problems of evil and suffering. The overall effort should provide believers with greater knowledge, clarity and assurance regarding their Christian faith."

Gary R. Habermas, Liberty Baptist Theological Seminary

CHRISTIAN CONFIDENCE

An Introduction to Defending the Faith

Chris Sinkinson

IVP Books

An imprint of InterVarsity Press
Downers Grove, Illinois

InterVarsity Press
P.O. Box 1400, Downers Grove, IL 60515-1426
Internet: www.ivpress.com
E-mail: email@ivpress.com

InterVarsity Press® is the book-publishing division of InterVarsity Christian Fellowship/USA®,
a movement of students and faculty active on campus at hundreds of universities, colleges and
schools of nursing in the United States of America, and a member movement of the International
Fellowship of Evangelical Students. For information about local and regional activities, write
Public Relations Dept., InterVarsity Christian Fellowship/USA, 6400 Schroeder Rd., P.O. Box
7895, Madison, WI 53707-7895, or visit the IVCF website at <www.intervarsity.org>.

While all stories in this book are true, some names and identifying information in this book have
been changed to protect the privacy of the individuals involved.

Cover design: Cindy Kiple

ISBN 978-0-8308-3786-2

Printed in the United States of America ∞

 InterVarsity Press is committed to protecting the environment and to the responsible
use of natural resources. As a member of Green Press Initiative we use recycled
paper whenever possible. To learn more about the Green Press Initiative, visit
<www.greenpressinitiative.org>.

Library of Congress Cataloging-in-Publication Data
A catalog record for this book is available from the Library of Congress.

P	17	16	15	14	13	12	11	10	9	8	7	6	5	4	3	2	1
Y	26	25	24	23	22	21	20	19	18	17	16	15	14	13	12

To Ros, Thomas and Toby

Contents

Acknowledgments

Everything that matters to me I have learned from others. Some people directly, some indirectly, have encouraged me to become a Christian and be persuaded of the trustworthiness of what God has said. It all started with Nick Pollard of Damaris, Josh McGregor of L'Abri Fellowship and Gavin D'Costa of Bristol University who gave me depth after my conversion. Along the way, numerous thoughtful friends have played a part in what has become this book.

I seem to have always had jobs that have permitted the opportunity to debate and discuss my faith with others. Numerous Christian Unions around the south-west of England and churches in Canterbury, Bath, Bournemouth and Alderholt have all been generous in allowing me time to pursue other avenues and sharpen my faith.

I must thank the students of Moorlands College, Christchurch, who have sat through hours of lectures and discussions, for their more direct input into this work. I am also grateful to the congregation of Alderholt Evangelical Congregational Church, who have given me space to be a reflective pastor. Helpful comment and corrections on various sections of the book came from Dr Stephen Catto, Professor

Alan Millard and Dr Philip Duce. The IVP staff have been a constant source of encouragement and guidance, particularly Eleanor Trotter and Kath Stanton for their careful work on the manuscript. Any errors or omissions are obviously my own mistakes! And then there was a little book called *The Last Battle* which I picked up before I became a Christian, and that got me thinking . . .

Introduction

Is Christianity in decline or on the march? In Western Europe and across America this is a difficult question to answer. In some places churches are growing and multiplying, while in other places they are withering and closing. In education, television and lecture halls Christianity is often put on the defensive. Objections to faith seem to multiply, and Christians can end up feeling embarrassed about their beliefs.

This is not a book about church growth, but it is a book written with the conviction that Christians should be confident in their faith.

This confidence is not arrogance, nor is it simple-mindedness. It is a confidence in what God has done and said that motivates our conversations. We have a faith grounded in real history, a faith that makes sense of life, and that has great appeal.

So how should this confidence shape the way we share our faith?

In this book I want to reflect on the history of Christian witness and what we can learn that will help us to sharpen our witness. You may be the practical type who just wants to get on with the job. You want a book that will give you a quick potted guide to answering difficult questions. This is not quite that book. But whether you are the practical type or a reflective thinker, I would like you to slow down and take some time to think these things through. How do we reason? What makes a good argument? Where have Christians gone wrong in history and why? You may find these questions a little abstract but we do need to ask them. Asking them will help us develop firmer foundations for faith and witness. You are not embarking on a quick read or an easy subject, but you are engaging with some of the most important themes in life. So join me in a journey through history, philosophy and theology, and see if we are more confident in our faith at the end!

Chris Sinkinson
August 2011

1. Apology for apologetics

Always tell the truth; that way you don't have to remember what you said.
Mark Twain

This is a book about something theologians call 'apologetics'. That sounds like the art of apologizing but is nothing of the sort.

The English word 'apology' is derived from a Greek word, *apologia*, which appears several times in various forms in the original text of the New Testament. To find out what the word means we can look at how it is translated in various places.

Peter encourages his readers to 'always be prepared to give an answer [*apologia*] to everyone who asks you to give the reason for the hope that you have' (1 Peter 3:15). A Christian should be ready and willing to give some kind of explanation for their faith when someone raises a question or objection. The Greek is formed from two words: *apo* (away) and *logos* (word), and together they mean something like giving a word back to someone who questions us. An apologetic is a 'word back' or a spoken defence for the Christian faith.

Outside of the Bible the word was used to describe what

happened in a court of law. The defence an accused person would present in court was their *apologia*. The Greek philosopher Plato wrote an account of the trial of his teacher entitled 'The Apology of Socrates'. Socrates did not say sorry, but he did defend his teachings and behaviour. In the New Testament, Luke describes Paul doing something similar as he stood before King Agrippa on unspecified charges: 'Paul motioned with his hand and began his defence [*apologia*]' (Acts 26:1).[1] Paul then presents various evidences for his conversion to follow Christ and his commission to share this faith throughout the region. Paul is so convinced of his evidence that he even hopes it may persuade the king to become a Christian too!

Paul came to use the word generally as a description of sharing the faith. He described himself as 'defending [*apologia*] and confirming the gospel' (Philippians 1:7).[2] In the New Testament period the Christian message was strongly opposed, both by the religious and the secular world. This opposition could take an intellectual or physical form. Apologetics is not much use against physical opposition, but it is the appropriate response to intellectual challenges. If someone threatens us with a baseball bat it is wiser to run, but if they challenge us with a question it is better to talk!

Christianity has had a long and noble tradition of reasonable defence. One of the earliest theological works produced after the completion of the New Testament was by Justin Martyr (c. AD 100–167) and simply called *The Apologies*. Since most of us are not Greek speakers, some may question the wisdom of continuing to use this word to describe what we do. However, apologetics has become an established branch of Christian thought. I will continue to use the word in order to draw on this tradition and remind us that Christianity has always offered a confident proclamation of the gospel to a doubting world.

Apologetics is sometimes treated as a specialized discipline or subject. However, it is important to recognize how closely it is related to the other things Christians do. We can consider apologetics in relation to evangelism, theology and philosophy. Theology provides the subject matter for apologetics (what we believe). Philosophy provides guidelines for what is rational (why we believe). Evangelism is the purpose of apologetics (how to help others to believe).

The relationship of apologetics to theology is very important. Theology enables us to clarify what the Bible teaches about God. Without good theology, apologetics can run away with ideas that sound plausible but are certainly not biblical. As we will see later, this has often happened in the history of apologetics. Theology must not be twisted to make it more palatable or plausible.

Apologetics and evangelism

Apologetics is a dimension of evangelism. As the early Christians explained and shared their faith, they also had to respond to the various questions their hearers would raise. Had the disciples stolen the body of their crucified hero to claim a resurrection from the dead? Would the growth of Christianity undermine the stability of Roman society? Questions like these were understandable and they raised doubts. We sometimes forget how unlikely the resurrection of Jesus from the dead would have seemed to the first hearers. The witnesses to the empty tomb were trembling and bewildered,[3] Thomas the apostle refused to believe it,[4] and the pagan Greeks sneered at Paul's faith in it.[5] Far from being a naïve and simplistic society ready to believe in anything, the world at the time of the New Testament was as sceptical as any. Objections were raised from the very beginning.

The early Christians had answers to those questions, and this was part of their apology. Over the course of the years the questions or objections changed, and so too did the kinds of answers that Christians gave. Sometimes false or misleading answers were given by Christians. Other, better, answers became almost the standard replies in the centuries that followed. Good or bad, apologetics describes the practice of Christians trying to present the case for their faith. On the whole, Christianity has always offered a robust and confident response to the objections of the world.

Any good defensive military campaign must also involve an offensive. Simply to defend a position indefinitely is likely to lead to failure unless support arises from elsewhere. The besieged castle cannot put up a defence for ever – it only holds out in the hope that reinforcements will eventually arrive to lead an attack. Apologetics is more than answering objections, more than defending the faith from its critics. Apologetics also means explaining how Christianity answers the questions of life and even pointing out where rival ideas are mistaken. So apologetics involves both defence and offence. But no Christian should want to be offensive in an unattractive way. However, we should want to point out why an alternative religion or ideology is at some point flawed or incomplete. In so doing, we may indeed offend a friend, because we are treading on beliefs that may matter a great deal to them. We need to make our case with humility and love. It is not our intention to offend, but it should be our aim to expose the limitations of any rival to Christ.

These defensive and offensive aspects of sharing our faith are sometimes called 'positive and negative apologetics'.[6] Paul went on the offensive as he shared his faith. He writes, 'We demolish arguments and every pretension that sets itself up against the knowledge of God' (2 Corinthians 10:5). He did not demolish or crush people, but he did demolish and undermine rival beliefs and faiths. No doubt a lot of people were offended. But we also know that many were persuaded. Paul was a confident Christian.

Some Christians give the impression that to explain the gospel is nothing more than sharing a few simple statements of faith – a few spiritual laws – which the hearer can either accept or reject. Sometimes this is enough. But usually more is required. We have all had the experience of sharing our faith and feeling as if we were speaking an alien language. Do our friends really understand what we are saying? Do they have questions about what we really mean? Do they want to know why we believe these statements are true? If we really love those we speak to then we will want to communicate clearly and effectively. This is why evangelism should always have apologetic content. We may not all be intellectuals or use long words, but we should be able to give a defence of our faith.

Famously, Charles Spurgeon once commented, 'Defend the Bible? I'd rather defend an uncaged lion!' In a sense the Bible needs no defence, and the truth of the gospel is found in its own authority. Apologetics puts the spotlight, not on the inadequacies of what God has said but on the inadequacies of our own sinful minds. It is because we often communicate the gospel *badly* that we need to improve. Our friends misunderstand us so we need to help them. The non-Christian philosopher Aristotle recognized this problem when he said, 'Every failure of Truth to persuade reflects the weakness of its advocates.'[7] The Truth does not need defending but it does need to be presented clearly – something apologetics will help us to do. We can find plenty of examples of reasoned defence of the Christian faith in the sermons and writings of Charles Spurgeon.

Apologetics is persuasive evangelism that engages with the real issues of the day. Many of the questions and objections we encounter will have been shaped by current ideas, morality and events. A recent terrorist outrage might make people think that religions are the cause of war. An immoral president or prime minister might convince many that Christianity is hypocritical. New discoveries in science could undermine confidence in the reliability of the Bible.

By contrast, the good news of Christianity never changes. The message foretold in the prophets of the Old Testament was revealed in the life of Jesus. That same message was explained and shared by the apostles and has since been handed down by faithful believers for two thousand years. This is the unchanging core of the Christian faith. However, we have a responsibility to communicate this truth to a changing world. Many of the questions of today are different from those asked centuries ago. Aspects of Christianity that were easily understood or assumed to be true by most of the population of Western Europe a hundred years ago are now thrown wide open to dispute and confusion.

A good example of this would be the biblical concept of judgment. Many people today struggle with the idea of eternal punishment because we have lost the sense of punishment being an irreversible penalty. In the contemporary world a prison can be called a corrective facility because punishment is supposed to help people change their ways. The idea of an irreversible punishment is no longer readily accepted. Therefore, the concepts of sin, judgment and eternal punishment need more defence and clarification. There are objections to these doctrines today that were not being raised by previous generations. An apologist is a Christian who believes it is important to be up to date, not in order to be fashionable but to press the case for Christianity at exactly the point where it is in dispute.

Paul was sensitive to the issues of his day. He was absolutely persuaded of the message he had to share. But he also took time to listen to, learn from and engage with the people he wanted to reach. In Athens, among the pagan philosophers, Paul tells his hearers, 'I walked around and looked carefully at your objects of worship' (Acts 17:23). Paul was not a tourist collecting souvenirs. Nor was he a neutral observer gathering facts to write up as a research project. Paul was an evangelist. He wanted to understand a rival worldview so that he could share his own faith more effectively in that setting. The sermon that followed is one of the most powerful examples of apologetics. Paul took time to look at the architecture of Athens, visit its temples and read its poets. He was not threatened by pagan culture, but engaged with it in order to communicate more effectively. We need to do the same thing to be effective in our own evangelism.

An apologist is not engaging in a unique ministry among Christians; rather this is an aspect of every Christian's witness. Of course some will be better at it than others. Some have a great ability to use logic, remember facts or think on their feet, and may therefore be particularly capable of defending the faith. Clearly Paul was one of these people. In the contemporary world we find examples in William Lane Craig, Ravi Zacharias, Alister McGrath and the late Francis Schaeffer. These individuals are called 'apologists' as they have particular gifts in using apologetics in their ministry. However, it is not always helpful to single out these people as apologists, because we are *all* called when a non-believer questions us to give a reason for the hope that we have. Explaining and defending our faith is a responsibility shared by all believers. And a failure to include apologetics in our conversations can create shallow conversions and shaky disciples.

Apologetics and philosophy

Apologetics can benefit greatly from the discipline of philosophy. The Greek word from which the English word
'philosophy' is derived means 'love of wisdom'. Philosophy
is used by practitioners of all faiths and none, so there are
Christian philosophers, Muslim philosophers, Marxist philosophers and atheist philosophers. Philosophy does not
dictate the content of belief (such as whether or not a god
exists), but philosophers do tend to agree on certain standards
for knowledge. Philosophy deals more with 'how' rather
than 'what' to think. We can usefully draw on philosophy to
make sense of our faith and communicate it persuasively.
But philosophers have no one insight or opinion on what
the truth may be. Someone once said that if you took all the
philosophers in the world and laid them end to end, you
still would not reach a conclusion! So the beliefs of philosophers are as diverse as those of the rest of the population.
But the way in which philosophers try to explain or debunk
ideas does find wide agreement. These are rules of logic and
reasoning without which communication breaks down.
The word 'logic' is derived from a Greek word *logos* which
means 'word', something that should remind us that logic is
an important element of using words. Illogical statements
may be considered nonsense; therefore some of these rules
are worth knowing if we are to communicate effectively. (We
will consider some of these rules in the next chapter.)

Limits of apologetics

Some philosophers arrogantly claim too much for their
discipline. We should not make the same mistake in our use
of apologetics. There are limitations in both what we can

know and how we understand what we know. Some things we just do not know. Other things we may believe but find it hard to explain or understand. While I am confident in my faith, I can certainly find it difficult to explain or meet objections that need to be carefully considered.

The Bible affirms this humble approach to knowledge in many ways. There is a genuine sense in which Christians realize that everything they know depends upon God. Having entered a living relationship with Christ, everything looks different now. Psalm 36:9 declares of God:

> With you is the fountain of life;
> in your light we see light.

Our vision is enhanced by the light of what God has revealed. The book of Job reflects on the humility of human understanding. Job asks where wisdom and understanding will be found and laments,

> It is hidden from the eyes of every living thing,
> concealed even from the birds of the air.
> (Job 28:21)

Job again reflects on the problem of vision. We cannot naturally see where true wisdom is found. Proverbs offers only one route to this wisdom:

> The fear of the LORD is the beginning of knowledge,
> but fools despise wisdom and discipline.
> (Proverbs 1:7)

Fear in this context means a proper respect for and acknowledgment of God. This is the humility required to find true knowledge. When Paul deals with the objections people might make to the sovereignty of God over history, he responds with the rebuke: 'Who are you, O man, to talk back to God?' (Romans 9:20). There will be many questions that we cannot easily answer, but our trust in God's wisdom remains firm.

So how does this call to humility in matters of knowledge bear on apologetics? No-one needs to be a Christian in order to make sense of every aspect of life. Plenty of non-Christians have been capable scientists, teachers and artists. But the Bible emphasizes wisdom over knowledge. Truly to make sense of the facts that we can see, and understand their spiritual significance, requires a dependence upon God and a willingness to listen. Apologetics cannot prove anything to a resistant or stubborn heart, for example. Many people may have a lot of knowledge but little spiritual wisdom.

Some believers worry about apologetics because they think it encourages a spirit of argumentativeness and confrontation. Jesus said, 'Blessed are the peacemakers' (Matthew 5:9), and the epistles call us to live at peace (see Hebrews 12:14). Questioning the beliefs of non-Christians can seem unfriendly and intolerant. The fruit of the Holy Spirit include peace and gentleness. Would we not be better living quiet lives of loving peace and trusting that God would use that witness to bring our friends to faith?

Perhaps the reason for this worry is found in the many bad examples of apologetics. Some Christians are argumentative. Some are rude about non-Christians. Some lose their temper or possess arrogant personalities. However, we can also find bad examples of preaching and evangelism. Some preaching is sloppy, incoherent or boastful. But the fact that there are bad examples does not mean that it should not or cannot be done well. Peter, in the passage we quoted earlier, goes on to tell his readers how to give a word back when questioned: 'But do this with gentleness and respect, keeping a clear conscience, so that those who speak maliciously against your good behaviour in Christ may be ashamed of their slander (1 Peter 3:15–16). There is never an excuse to be rude or aggressive, whether we are parking our car or explaining our faith. Christian love should characterize all that we do. As we explain our faith we should be humble, admitting to things we don't know or to questions we find difficult. We should be respectful, questioning alternative beliefs without mocking them. We should be gentle, knowing that winning someone's interest in Christ is more important than winning an argument.

James Sire makes many astute comments on why good arguments often fail.[8] It is not enough to have an argument that is valid. We need grace, humility, thoughtfulness and integrity in our presentation of the Christian faith. Without such grace a valid argument may be entirely ineffective. Nonetheless, such graces are compatible with a willingness to enter the fray and confront false beliefs and arguments against Christ. In the Sermon on the Mount, Jesus said blessed are the 'peacemakers' not the 'peace lovers'. The Christian is not called to do anything for a quiet life and avoid controversy. He or she is called to get into the thick of it, bringing truth and direction in a world of deception and darkness. We make peace in the world through a confident and robust explanation of our faith and an enquiring exploration of the alternatives. The only peace that lasts is the peace with God that comes through faith in him. So a peacemaking Christian cannot be afraid of controversy.

This brings us to another important worry about the role of apologetics. Do we really believe that we can argue someone into the kingdom of heaven? Is becoming a Christian a matter of being convinced intellectually? Can apologetics actually convert people? At one level this is no different from asking whether or not someone can be preached or talked into the kingdom of heaven. The fact that Christians do a lot of preaching and talking does not mean that we think our preaching or talking does the converting. A Christian believes that conversion is more than just forming an opinion about some facts. Conversion is a supernatural event – a miracle. It is a work of God, through the Holy Spirit, to open someone's mind and heart so that they trust in Jesus as their personal Saviour and Lord.[9] Sharing our personal testimony, explaining a Bible passage or answering objections are all valid things to do, but without a sovereign work of the Holy Spirit none of them is able to convert anyone. God uses various means to do his will. He uses a personal testimony, a kind deed or a reasonable argument to create a climate favourable to faith. Whether our friend actually becomes a Christian or not is out of our hands.

Apologetics is singled out for this worry because it can be understood to imply too much confidence in human reason. One of Josh McDowell's works on the resurrection of Christ has as its subtitle: 'Compelling evidence which proves the resurrection of Jesus Christ beyond reasonable doubt'.[10] This confidence is not without its problems, and some Christians are deeply suspicious of traditional apologetics for claiming a neutral standard of reason. Brian McLaren has been a significant critic of the idea that apologetics should be a defence of the faith. He gives various reasons for this, including the concern that apologetics treats friends as enemies and exaggerates the case for Christianity. These reasons do apply to some bad examples but certainly cannot be a blanket criticism of all robust apologetics. However, underlying McLaren's view is a more serious issue. He argues that apologetics too often assumes 'absolute knowledge'.[11] While he accepts that there is such a thing as absolute truth, he denies that we can ever know this truth in an absolute way. Therefore, our task is not to offer 'answers' but to offer 'mysteries'.[12] McLaren's objections do not fit well with the proper confidence we find among Bible characters and authors. It is fair to admit that our knowledge of the truth is incomplete, sometimes faulty and open to change. But we *are* entitled to confidence and we *can* offer answers to many of the awkward questions we are asked. This is not arrogance on our part; rather it is assurance that God has not wanted to leave his purposes shrouded in mystery but has revealed them to us. Consider the confidence of Paul who writes of the resurrection: 'If Christ has not been raised, our preaching is useless and so is your faith' (1 Corinthians 15:14). A Christian is entitled, even compelled, to hold this humble confidence. As we will see when we discuss the nature of faith, a Christian should be confident in the central claims of Christianity. This is not because we are overconfident in human reason, but because we have faith in God's revelation. To distrust all absolute knowledge is to distrust God's faithfulness in revelation.

However, as we close this chapter it is right to respond to critics like McLaren by acknowledging some of the limitations of apologetics. We are more than just detached minds. We are complex creatures formed, in some entangled way, of reason, emotions, will, imagination and desires. Jesus called us to 'love the Lord [our] God with all [our] heart and with all [our] soul and with all [our] mind and with all [our] strength' (Mark 12:30). In these words he confronts our entire life with the call to discipleship. Apologetics does not address every area of life. Apologetics is only one strand of discipleship and should work hand in hand with other forms of evangelism and service. People certainly do have intellectual needs, but they also have physical and emotional needs for material assistance and counselling.

Apologetics will also be limited by our own meagre understanding. We do not have all the answers. Old Testament Israelites were clearly told that God would give them all they needed to know but not everything they might *want* to know (Deuteronomy 29:29). We need to know how to live a life that pleases God and how to enjoy him for eternity. We may also want to know why a particular way of life pleases God or what the new, eternal creation will be like. But many questions will simply go beyond what we can possibly know. Furthermore, we do not fully know all that God has revealed in the Bible, and we learn new things with the passage of time and realize that we were ignorant or had misunderstood what the Bible taught. We easily forget what we should have learned and are often stumped at questions people pose. This is not an excuse for laziness or shallow thinking. It is a humble admission that our defence of the faith will often stumble over our own intellectual limitations.

The effectiveness of apologetics is also limited by the fact that belief is more than just logical assent. There are many reasons why people hold the beliefs they do. Many factors influence us as we grow up, and these can be more persuasive than logic. Prejudice and subtle influences in our upbringing can have an impact on who we are most likely to listen to. Our commitments to family, jobs and friendships will sway us. Physical constraints to do with our health, our worries or a lack of time will dictate many of our beliefs. Our imagination and aesthetic tastes will also give us a bias towards certain beliefs. When we present arguments for our faith, we must be aware of these powerful forces exercising their influences over both ourselves and our hearers. The imagination can soften the mind to explore the Christian message. Many people were awakened to an interest in Christianity through the imaginative literature of C. S. Lewis and J. R. R. Tolkien.

Their stories made the Christian worldview an attractive option to explore further in terms of apologetics. But there is of course a reverse side to this use of the imagination. An author such as Philip Pullman can use imaginative literature to make an appealing case for atheism. Arguments are not made with content alone but with the way that content is presented.

Furthermore, reason and logic are themselves limited. Many important beliefs and commitments that we hold are beyond the realms of logical analysis. Loving relationships, experiences of faith and the revelation of God's character should not be illogical, but they can certainly go beyond logic. Perhaps Mr Spock would tell someone that his desire to marry his fiancée was only logical, but most of us realize that there are many underlying factors beyond logic in the beliefs we hold and the choices we make. It may be logical to love someone and want to marry them, but it is not only logical. There are reasons of the heart and will that cannot be simply stated in terms of logic. We have longings, attachments and attractions that will influence some of our most significant decisions.

It certainly does not follow that religious faith is nothing more than an emotional feeling or artistic taste. We are still dealing in the realms of fact. But there are facts about the universe itself which do not readily fit in with conventional reason. Quantum mechanics and the theory of relativity do not seem common sense but have observational proofs in their favour. No wonder one scientific journal referring to some of the counter-intuitive implications of quantum mechanics carried a cartoon with the caption: 'After Quarks, the virgin birth is a doddle!' Common sense and abstract logic are useful in certain areas of life but not in *every* area of life. Even in understanding atoms and black holes our common sense can be baffled. It should not surprise us therefore that our understanding of God will be partial and sometimes beyond simple logical description. The doctrine of the Trinity is not illogical but remains difficult to state in simple, rational statements. But given that God is eternal and all-powerful that should hardly surprise us! The Bible itself is not a revelation of rational statements but a description, through historical stories and events, of a God we can only partly understand.

These limitations of apologetics should encourage the right spirit of dependence on God in our life and witness. Without the presence of the Spirit of God all our efforts at persuasion will prove futile. Even when we answer objections or explain the reasons for our faith, we are humble in admitting our own questions and difficulties. This dependence and humility encourages prayer. We pray for wisdom, guidance and the right words as we try to explain our faith. We also pray for those to whom we are talking. Sometimes these may be the immediate prayers offered as we are about to speak (i.e. Nehemiah 2:4), but presumably such prayers are offered only because they are part of a more general lifestyle where prayer is the bedrock (Nehemiah 1:4). Effective apologetics should be bathed in this kind of prayerfulness.

Christian apologetics should be spiritual, humble, truthful and effective. We should never divide confidence and humility. Confident Christianity can be robust in its defence of the truthfulness of faith while also being gracious in how that faith is shared.

2. Apologetics and philosophy

It is true that a little philosophy inclines man's mind to atheism; but depth in philosophy brings man's mind to religion.
Francis Bacon

Thinking straight

We have already seen that philosophy simply means the 'love of wisdom'. It does not teach any particular doctrine or truth. Rather, there are many different philosophies. All the major religions offer their own philosophy. It is pointless for someone to introduce a statement by saying, 'Philosophy teaches . . .' or 'Philosophers have proven . . .' Philosophers contradict one another on almost every issue. Sometimes they almost seem to contradict one another for the sheer pleasure of it! When Paul warned the Colossians against 'hollow and deceptive philosophy', he was not dismissing the value of any kind of philosophy, only the kind of sham philosophy that depended on 'human tradition and the basic principles of this world'.[1]

It is encouraging to know how many Christian philosophers there have been. Indeed, Christians have been prominent in the secular philosophy departments of universities for many decades. While atheism has plenty of vocal support, Christian philosophers include Richard Swinburne, Paul Helm, Terence Penelhum, Basil Mitchell, Alvin Plantinga and Thomas V. Morris.[2]

Philosophy, as we know, does not provide one set of agreed conclusions. However, the particular discipline of philosophy does offer some guidance on how to think. Over the centuries philosophers have debated and defined the terms involved in what makes a good argument. By 'a good argument' they do not mean a blazing row. A good argument is simply a plausible case made for something we believe. Opponents in a debate may concede that their partner has some good arguments, even if they do not agree with them. In apologetics we want to present our faith as persuasively as possible, and to do so we can learn much from philosophy.

The first term we need to understand is 'logic'. A good argument should be logical. A bad argument is illogical. Logic functions in apologetics just like grammar does for language. If we want to communicate well, then we consider the grammar of our sentences. Most of the time this is sub-conscious. But sometimes we realize that our failure to be grammatical has led to a misunderstanding. The restaurant that boasted, 'It takes many ingredients to make our meals great, but our secret ingredient is our customers' left itself open to a grisly misreading. Likewise, some famous newspaper headlines have been liable to misunderstanding:

- Iraqi Head seeks Arms
- Miners Refuse to Work after Death
- Squad Helps Dog Bite Victim

An ungrammatical sentence is not a false sentence. Likewise, a grammatical sentence may not be a true sentence. Grammar simply clarifies meaning. The same principle applies to logic and arguments. A logical argument is one that is presented with clarity. Whether it is true or false will depend on other factors.

To understand logic we need to distinguish between what philosophers call a premise and what they call an argument. A premise is a statement of fact, such as 'It is raining.' This might be true or false. The example premise is one we could easily test by observing the weather. Christianity has many beliefs which can be premises, such as 'God exists', 'Jesus is the Son of God' and 'The Bible is the Word of God.' These premises may be true or false. An argument is a way in which we might try to present a case for our beliefs. For example, 'God exists because the Bible tells us so.' The linking word 'because' indicates that we are reading an argument. Logic applies to the argument, so we may well ask, 'Is this argument logical?' Notice the limitations of what we are asking. We are not actually asking here, 'Is this belief true?' No, that is a much wider question, settled in many different ways.

An argument could be logical but based on false premises. Or it could be illogical but based on premises that are true. Take, 'Dogs are carnivores because the Bible is the Word of God.' The first premise (dogs are carnivores) and the second (the Bible is the Word of God) may both be true, but the argument is obviously unsound. One does not follow on from the other. Logic is useful for sorting out whether or not our arguments make sense. In this last case the statement is an example of what philosophers call a 'non sequitur' (Latin for 'does not follow').

Apologists should be concerned with logic. Of course, logic is not everything. Logic does not prove that our starting point or premises are true. It does not always apply in a simple way to real-world experience. Sometimes we struggle to express our beliefs verbally and recognize the limitations of language and logic. But logic remains of great importance for weighing up the value of the case we are making for faith and rethinking how we state that case.

Philosophers like to break down arguments into a simple logical form, often two premises and a conclusion. An example might be the following:

Premise 1: Jesus was a person.
Premise 2: All people are sinners.
Conclusion: Therefore Jesus was a sinner.

This conclusion is fairly widely held, for many people do assume Jesus sinned, and an argument like this is probably lurking somewhere in the background of the thinking of those who hold it. Stated this way, the argument is logical. However, an orthodox Christian would want to ask where the argument goes wrong, given that they are unhappy with the conclusion. The problem is found somewhere in the second premise. Though the Bible does say, 'All have sinned and fall short of the glory of God' (Romans 3:23), we take this to mean all ordinary people in ordinary circumstances that we see around us today. It does not imply that 'all people must necessarily be sinners in any circumstances'. The first people created by God, for example, were not originally sinners. People living in the new creation or in heaven are not sinners. Therefore, the God who became a man in Jesus could both be a person and be sinless. Through this kind of consideration we realize that premise number two was being misused and was playing on an ambiguity in our language. Not only do we identify why the argument goes wrong, but we also clarify what we mean by words like 'person' and 'sinner'.

Over two thousand years ago the philosopher Aristotle proposed that there were three basic laws of logic, and his claim has stood the test of time. The first is the law of identity, which simply states that something is itself. If it is true that God exists, then God exists. This may not sound particularly profound, but it is a very basic logical law.

A second logical law is called the law of 'excluded middle', which implies that there is no 'middle position' between something being true and something being false. So if we consider the claim 'God exists', then either God does exist and the statement is true, or God does not exist and the statement is not true. The middle position is excluded.

The third law is the principle of non-contradiction. This means that we cannot hold two contradictory statements to be true at the same time. For example, it would be a contradiction to say, 'I exist' and 'I do not exist' at the same moment. Of course, in everyday life we can find plenty of exceptions. It is possible to believe that 'it is raining' and 'it is not raining' on a showery day. However, this example demonstrates the rule: we know that we must carefully qualify what we mean, by explaining things further. We cannot believe, 'It is not raining in any sense whatsoever here and now', while also believing, 'It is raining very clearly and heavily right here and right now', without breaking the rule of non-contradiction. All the exception tells us is that there are situations where we need to explain ourselves more clearly.

These three principles are not only basic, simple rules of logic; they are also crucial to good communication. If we want to be clear communicators then we will bear them in mind. However, these principles can sound quite abstract and unsuitable for dealing with our complex lives and universe. In the modern world people often talk of 'fuzzy logic'. Fuzzy logic was developed among engineers in the 1960s to deal with matters that involve approximations rather than exact statements. Obviously in real-life situations there are many circumstances where a statement is not true or false, but might lie somewhere in between. To say, 'The king is bald' could be true or false, or, depending on how little hair counts as baldness, could be somewhere in between. Fuzzy logic helped technicians develop machinery that could take into account real-world situations which were not so black and white. It has been relevant to car braking systems and music players too. For many reasons we find people dismissive of the value of logic. Life involves matters of degree and interpretation that do not fit into neat boxes of right or wrong, true or false.

However, fuzzy logic does not imply that basic logical laws are not valid. It simply provides a way of taking into account the fact that some complex ideas are hard to state in brief, logical terms. Take the principle of non-contradiction for example. If I say, 'Bruce is married', then this statement implies, 'It is not true to say, "Bruce is unmarried."' That sounds simple enough. However, in real-world situations we may point out many complications. Perhaps Bruce is a Roman Catholic who is seeking to have his marriage annulled and declared invalid. In this case, Bruce will be able to declare that in the eyes of the church he was never married at all. However, in legal terms he *has* been married. Or perhaps Bruce is living with his partner and in legal terms has a 'common-law marriage', even though this has not been recognized in religious terms. Now Bruce declares that he is not married but would like to be married. Or perhaps Bruce and his partner have split up, and he then says that his marriage is only on paper. There are many real-life situations that can complicate a statement, including what exactly we mean by our words and the context in which we are using them.

But none of this discussion implies that logical laws are not valid. It simply demonstrates that communication involves explanation. Given all the factors that we need to take into account when we try to understand what someone is saying, the three principles still hold. In fact, if someone were to claim that 'Bruce is married and unmarried', then the onus would be upon them to explain how such a statement could be true. They may be able to do so, but in order to communicate they will still be relying on the principles we have described.

Recognizing the value of logic in communication, we can then draw upon many helpful insights that philosophers have made over the years. For example, when we think about arguments in their logical form, we can see more clearly when they go wrong. Invalid arguments are called fallacies. They can be very subtle, and some appear regularly in debates and dialogues. It is useful to know some of them in order to avoid committing them whenever we can.

You must be mistaken!

Many different fallacies have been identified over the years. Aristotle identified thirteen, and they have been generally accepted ever since. Some are more formal, logical fallacies which we will not deal with here. Instead, we will consider the more simple informal fallacies that are in common currency. An informal fallacy is a general logical mistake that is found in ordinary conversation. Many of them are given Latin names which helps to give them an appearance of technical precision.

Ad hominem

Ad hominem means 'to the person' and applies to arguments that attack the person rather than the grounds for their beliefs.

In debates, someone might seek to discredit the claims their opponent is making, for example, by pointing out their lack of education, their moral failings or their undesirable associations. This kind of argument distracts us from the evidences themselves and undermines the truth claim, for unrelated reasons. 'God does not exist, because those who have a religious experience of God are naïve and gullible' commits this fallacy. Even if it *could* be shown that all Christians are naïve believers, this would still not disprove the claim that God exists. In the Gospels we find that some people dismissed the messianic claims of Jesus because of his home town ('Nazareth! Can anything good come from there?'; John 1:46), his lineage and his association with sinners (Matthew 11:18–19). These could all be examples of dismissing a truth claim for unrelated reasons. The fallacy is also buried in a statement such as, 'The Prime Minister is only in favour of raising taxes for the rich because he comes from a poor family.'

A mirror image of this fallacy is found in the appeal to authority or the appeal to the majority. This is where we might back up our argument simply by appealing to irrelevant but remarkable qualifications; a surgeon's opinions on health-care are worth listening to but his opinions on the textual reliability of the Bible may or may not be relevant. Similarly, if we claim that something is true because 'everyone knows . . . ' or 'most people think . . . ', then we may be committing the fallacy of appealing to the majority. In the thirteenth century most people thought the sun revolved around the earth, but it was later found that most people were actually mistaken.

There are some contexts where an appeal to a person's character is relevant – when someone is a witness in a court of law for example, we expect them to be generally trust-worthy. Evidence against their trustworthiness will undermine any evidence they are supplying in the legal case. Therefore a statement such as, 'This person is not a good choice of character witness because she has a habit of telling lies' would be a valid argument. The person's misbehaviour is relevant evidence against her reliability as a character witness. This is not an argument against the truth of what she claims or believes, but an argument against her credibility. This is relevant to Christian apologetics too when we are providing personal testimony. If we are generally unreliable or prone to fantasy, then it is only fair that others may question our credibility. Likewise, if we are prone to believing ridiculous things or telling lies, then why would anyone ever believe our claims about Jesus or the Bible? This is a fair challenge, but the ad hominem fallacy is being committed when people dismiss religious beliefs by trying to discredit the believer's reputation. Christians should provide as little ammunition for detractors as possible, despite the fallacious nature of such arguments.

Begging the question

This fallacy is present where the point someone is trying to prove is already being assumed in their argument. In effect, the person is begging us to accept the answer even before the argument is given. This kind of fallacy can appear in what are called 'circular arguments'. A common example is, 'The Bible is the Word of God because the Bible teaches that God gave us the Bible.' In this example, we have to assume the Bible is the Word of God in order to see the evidence that it is the Word of God. If we don't accept that the Bible is the Word of God, then we do not need to accept what the Bible may claim about itself.

Not every circular argument is a fallacy, however, and it is possible that every argument about matters of ultimate concern will in some sense be circular. Arguments about the nature of existence, mathematics and even the basis of logic itself are in some ways dependent on themselves. But how do we know if a fallacy is illogical? Only by a circular argument! We must make assumptions about reality in order to be able to talk about reality. So a Christian need not be embarrassed that some basic beliefs appear to beg the question. However, if we care about presenting helpful reasons for our faith, we will try to avoid circular arguments wherever possible.

Another simple example might appear in ethical debates like this:

Abortion is murder.
Murder is wrong.
Abortion is wrong.

The argument seems valid, but it is an example of begging the question. The critic will question the premise: why should we think that abortion is murder? So the defender of the claim 'abortion is wrong' will be more careful to define what murder is and how abortion counts as a form of murder. The defender benefits from this exchange because it encourages him to present a more convincing argument. This reminds us that sometimes a circular argument is valid but unpersuasive. It is not enough for an apologist to present valid arguments; he also needs to present persuasive arguments!

Equivocation

This can be a deliberate or an accidental confusion of terms which have multiple meanings. By confusing the terms, an argument can sound persuasive even though it is completely baseless. Such arguments commit 'ambiguity fallacies' because they rely on multiple meanings of words to make their point. A simple example is this:

A cheap burger is better than nothing.
Nothing is better than prime steak.
A cheap burger is better than prime steak.

We instantly know something is wrong with the argument but have to look twice to see what it is. The argument has played on the ambiguity of the word 'nothing' which means something different in each premise. A more complex example would be found in a simple claim such as, 'Jews, Christians and Muslims all worship God.' At one level this sounds perfectly reasonable. These are the three monotheistic faiths, and they all repudiate polytheism and make God the object of their devotion. But do they all worship the same God, as the statement implies? Or do they define God in terms of their own traditions and scriptures so that while there is considerable overlap it is not clear that the God they worship is actually the same? Furthermore, does worship mean the same thing in each tradition? One finds prayer and song and giving to the poor common to each religion, but is this what we mean by worship? Equivocation allows an arguer to slip from one meaning to another without changing vocabulary. It can be a crafty way of smuggling in a controversial conclusion, but with entirely uncontroversial observations.

A straw-man argument

Sometimes we want to dismiss a false belief and so we describe it in a way that is easy to disprove. This is tempting but it achieves nothing if no-one really holds the belief for those reasons. We have not defeated a real opponent, but only a man or woman of straw. People do this because it makes their own arguments sound more credible, but it actually adds nothing whatsoever to the logical value of what they are claiming. Let's consider an example: 'The Bible cannot be infallible because there are many occasions when we find inaccurate numbers being used to record populations and dates.' In this statement there is an example of equivocation in the use of the term 'inaccurate'. Does the critic really mean 'inexact' rather than 'inaccurate'? Numbers may be inexact without being inaccurate. The standard of accuracy varies depending on what we are talking about. However, underlying the statement is a straw-man argument. It suggests that those who hold to infallibility have never considered the matter of round numbers, approximate quantities, relative dating or even problems in the transmission of the text. Only a man of straw (someone who doesn't exist or at least is not relevant to this kind of debate) would hold such a simplistic view of the infallibility of the Bible. The argument can sound effective but, if the truth be told, it has only demolished a man of straw.

Genetic fallacy

Genetics traces the origins of organisms, and the genetic fallacy is an argument that plays on the origins of a belief. For example, 'People believe that God exists because of the longing they have for the loss of their childhood relationship to parents' may or may not be true, but it has no bearing on whether or not it is true that God exists. People might form beliefs for all sorts of strange reasons, and the beliefs they form could still be true. In ancient Greece the philosophers not only calculated that the earth was a sphere, but also argued for the existence of Australia. They did so on the basis that there had to be a land mass balancing the land mass of the known world in our part of the globe. You could say that they had a valid belief, but the reasons or origins of their belief were flawed. It commits the genetic fallacy to imply that the origins of a belief undermine the validity of a belief. The Greeks were not wrong to believe that the earth was a globe.

This argument is often used in the history of religions. It is possible to trace the development of religious thought over the centuries, and it is clear that most traditions have developed in sophistication with the way doctrines are understood. The genetic fallacy uses this historical observation to suggest that, if we can explain how a doctrine has developed or where it has come from, then we have proved that that doctrine is not valid. It is sometimes suggested that the doctrine of redemption through the death and resurrection of Jesus has developed from earlier mythological accounts of a dying and rising Redeemer God. But even if such a connection could be established, it would be a genetic fallacy to suggest that this disproves the doctrine of the atonement.

Etymological fallacy

Sometimes the historical origins or formation of a word are taken to prove its present-day use or meaning. But words are continually in development, and their present meaning may be unrelated to their historical origins. For example, the Greek word for 'power' found in the New Testament is *dynamis*, from which we get our modern English word 'dynamite'. However, it is a fallacy to then take from the modern meaning of dynamite, an explosive substance, an insight into what the New Testament writers intended. A related etymological fallacy is found in trying to break down the components of a word to discover its meaning – imagine what fun could be had in trying to understand what a 'butterfly' is merely from the meaning of the components 'butter' and 'fly'.

These fallacies are useful to know because they give us general patterns of argument that are unconvincing. Sometimes we can't quite put our finger on what it is that is wrong with an argument until we try to describe it as a type of fallacy. It is important to emphasize again that the conclusion of a fallacious argument may still be true. As an example, consider this:

> Roman Catholics often pray to the Virgin Mary.
> The Pope often prays to the Virgin Mary.
> Therefore the Pope is a Roman Catholic.

This is a fallacious argument even though the conclusion is true. For one thing, there are many people who often pray to the Virgin Mary who are not Roman Catholics. But more importantly, in this example it is not praying to the Virgin Mary that makes the Pope a Roman Catholic. You can usually spot a fallacy by substituting different terms that provide an absurd counter-example:

> Jehovah's Witnesses often carry Bibles.
> The Pope often carries a Bible.
> The Pope is a Jehovah's Witness.

Noticing fallacies is very useful for improving our own thinking about what we know and for engaging with critics. It is a rather negative practice: it doesn't really prove anything – it just clears away some of the rubbish.

Philosophy provides many useful tools for helping us to think straight. It is not the case that we can 'prove' every point of our faith in a way that everyone will find acceptable. The very fact that highly respected philosophers disagree over Christian beliefs shows that important matters cannot be settled simply by logic or proof. However, we should still make use of philosophy as a tool to help us sort out the way we present our case.

In providing a reason for our faith we must avoid fallacious arguments. We want to provide good reasons – whether from our experience, from history or from the nature of the universe. We want to respond to objections with relevant counter-examples. We do so not because we think we can make someone a Christian or even win arguments as an end in itself, but because valid reasoning makes our message clearer and more compelling.

Keep it simple

Fallacies are to be avoided. Understanding what they are will help us weed out unhelpful arguments and unclear communication. But what makes a good argument? Philosophers have identified some very helpful insights here too.

William of Ockham (1288–1347) was an English friar who wrote extensively on logic. He identified a principle since known as 'Occam's razor'. Occam's razor implies that the simplest solution is probably the correct one. This principle is a sharp razor to cut away unnecessary complications. So if we are trying to explain complex phenomena, then we tend to be attracted towards the explanation which involves the least number of assumptions. Oxford philosopher Richard Swinburne suggests that we all have an innate bias towards the simpler explanation. If I wake one morning to find an unknown car parked in the driveway, then I could imagine different explanations. Perhaps someone left the car there by mistake? The car might be a surprise gift from a wealthy relative. Or perhaps the car had spontaneously emerged into existence? Our innate bias is towards the simpler option, so we prefer the first explanation. Likewise, sightings of UFOs are more likely explained as atmospheric events or military test flights than actual alien visitors. It is important to note that Occam's razor cannot decide what is true or false. Perhaps those really were alien visitors who left their lights on when they flew over your house last night. But the principle of parsimony encourages us to seek the simplest possible explanation.

Occam's razor is often turned against Christianity. Take the resurrection of Jesus. For simplicity let us imagine we are deciding between two rival explanations. The first is that God ordained a supernatural miracle that brought a dead man back to life. The second is that the disciples told a lie and hoaxed his resurrection. Critics suggest that Occam's razor would declare the second explanation most simple and therefore most likely. This is in reality a misuse of the principle that plays on a sleight of hand. We should be suspicious of its popularity among atheists, given William of Ockham's own clear faith in a supernatural God. Consider the two explanations again. For the second to be true, we need to explain the problems surrounding the deceptive behaviour of the disciples. Why did they lie? What did they have to gain? Given that they were not expecting a physical resurrection, where did the idea originate? The second explanation is not simple. It can sound surprising, but the supernatural explanation is logically simple. The sleight of hand used by critics is that they play on the fallacy of equivocation. They take 'simple' to mean something like 'easier to believe', and given that they don't believe in God, the traditional explanation for the resurrection cannot be simple. They even give the impression that because God is complicated to understand he cannot be a part of any simple explanation. However, these worries have nothing to do with Occam's razor.

Let's take another example. Police arrive at a scene where a man is dead on the floor. The most obvious, immediate explanation is that he has died of a heart attack. However, on investigation, evidence emerges that he has been deliberately poisoned by a murderer. Is the second explanation too complex? It certainly involves more secondary considerations. It also involves the incredible complexity of another person. Given how complex persons are with their minds, motives and histories, this explanation could be considered ripe for Occam's razor. Of course, it isn't. The complexity of the murderer's personality does not affect the simplicity of the explanation.

'Simple' in Ockham's language meant that the number of factors involved should not be multiplied needlessly. Of course, the explanation for an event may not be the first one that occurs to us or the easiest to imagine – police investigations would be over in a few minutes if that counted as a strong argument. Nor must all the components of an explanation be simple: minds, machines and supernatural beings are not always easy to understand. All that Occam's razor indicates is that, all things being equal, the least number of assumptions the better. This is a helpful principle for apologetics. We should keep our arguments as straightforward and simple as possible.

In this chapter we have seen that Christians can indeed gain helpful insights from philosophy. There is no reason to be intimidated by grand, hostile claims some philosophers make. The reality is that philosophers argue with one another as much as with anyone else. The search for truth can only be aided by clear thinking and clear communication. Christians have had different attitudes to reason and apologetics, so we shall consider some of those now and see what we can learn from them.

3. Christian persuaders

*If I have seen further it is by standing on
the shoulders of giants.*
Isaac Newton

Christians have had quite different views on apologetics. They
ask fundamental questions about the role of reason in how we
come to faith. These are questions such as: What is the role of
the Holy Spirit in persuasion? How much does a non-Christian
already know about God before they read the Bible? In what
ways has God revealed himself apart from the Bible? The
answers to such questions will inevitably shape the way we
do apologetics.

But before we try to identify some of the Bible's teachings
on these questions, we'll look at the answers Christians have
given over the centuries. We can summarize these in terms
of three significant alternatives.[1] First, fideism which often
involves an outright rejection of apologetics as 'too rational'.
Secondly, evidentialism which is often thought to be the classic
approach to apologetics. Thirdly, Reformed apologetics,
an approach that has variations with rather intimidating
names like Reformed epistemology and presuppositionalism

but still remains very popular among evangelicals. Must we choose only one? Let's consider them all first and then come back to that question in the next chapter.

By faith alone

Fideism is a Christian approach that rejects traditional apologetics. The term is derived from the Latin word for 'faith' (*fides*). Fideists emphasize that the knowledge of God comes through faith in God alone. They claim that traditional apologetics panders to the arrogance of sinful humanity. Rational arguments are not the path of humble submission to the God of the Bible. Paul is sometimes understood as fideistic when he makes a claim like this:

> My message and my preaching were not with wise and persuasive words, but with a demonstration of the Spirit's power, so that your faith might not rest on men's wisdom, but on God's power.[2]

The greatest demonstration of the Spirit's power is the cross of Christ, and this gospel message is 'foolishness' to non-believers (1 Corinthians 1:18). The fideist implies that the basis of the Christian faith is inaccessible to reason. The first step to belief is faith. Over the centuries Tertullian, Augustine, Martin Luther and Karl Barth have been thought to teach some form of fideism. Augustine (354–430) wrote, 'No one is fit to find God, who does not first believe what he will afterwards learn to know.'[3] The most famous statement of this approach is sometimes attributed to Anselm (1033–1109), who described the knowledge of God as 'faith seeking understanding'. Faith comes first. Without faith, abstract reasoning cannot lead us to the knowledge of God. In the light of faith, our understanding and intellect are purified and transformed so that we can believe and make sense of spiritual reality.

We need to distinguish two forms of fideism. In its strongest form, fideism has no place at all for apologetics. Christians from this school of thought would have closed this book long ago – if they had even opened it in the first place! Some theologians have even gloried in their belief that faith contradicts reason. The more unreasonable their faith, the more virtuous it must be. Tertullian (AD 160–230) remarked, 'The Son of God died; it is by all means to be believed because it is absurd.' Believing in something in the teeth of the evidence could be seen as a mark of great faith. Such extreme fideism assumes faith and reason are in conflict and makes apparent absurdity a virtue. This reminds us of the words of Lewis Carroll when the Queen replies to Alice's denial that she can believe the impossible: 'I dare say you haven't had much practice . . . When I was your age, I always did it for half-an-hour a day. Why, sometimes I've believed as many as six impossible things before breakfast.'[4]

Many Christians in the contemporary world are influenced by some strong form of fideism. Some may sincerely believe that preaching has no need of reasons, evidences or persuasion. They simply trust that God will use their witness and overcome any obstacles to faith. Their sincerity is not in question. But others are just being lazy. They find the idea of apologetics too demanding and are afraid they will not be able to answer difficult questions that arise. They choose fideism to excuse themselves from having to take tricky questions seriously. There is nothing commendable in this kind of attitude, and it sets young believers up for failure when they encounter those awkward questions in later life.

However, there is a different form of fideism. It is true that faith is not the product of rational arguments, and faith supplies knowledge of things otherwise inaccessible to reason. But faith does not have to contradict reason. When Augustine claimed, 'I believe in order that I might understand' (Latin, *credo ut intelligam*), he was affirming that there are many beliefs that come before rational arguments. Reason has its place, but faith comes first, and reason follows. Faith provides the basis for trusting that there is an almighty God who has spoken his Word that we read in the Bible. Reason follows this faith commitment as we try to understand what that Word means. Fideists who argue thus are not making any excuses for intellectual laziness. They are providing a warning against unhealthy confidence in human reason. Regarding Anselm, who expressed his own theology as 'faith seeking under- standing', it has to be noted that he was very happy with rational, logical arguments: 'By "faith" Anselm did not mean a basic assent to the truth of Christianity, but an active love for God. It is this love of God that seeks to know God. *That* is faith seeking understanding.'[5]

After the Reformation in Europe, there were many Protest- ant theologians and pastors who developed very logical or rational systems of thought. Some Christians found this a sterile, arid environment in which to experience real spiritual life. Søren Kierkegaard (1813–55), the Danish philosopher, was particularly critical of what he saw as the dead orthodox Christian church of his day. He argued that Christianity was primarily a passionate and radical experience of commitment to Christ. Kierkegaard was sceptical of apologetics when it sought to make Christianity plausible. A plausible Christianity was not after all the faith of the Bible. However, it does not follow that Kierkegaard had no place for apologetics. He did. But his brand of apologetics emphasized the limitations of philosophy and human reason. Faith for him implied solid conviction, not just reasonable arguments. So Kierkegaard did offer reasons for faith, but he never allowed these to displace the priority of personal commitment: 'My firm conviction is higher than reasons: it is actually the conviction which sustains the reasons, not the reasons which sustain the convictions.'[6] Fideism is not irrational. The fideist knows that reason has its place, but that place is not in settling the question of whether or not God exists. That question is settled by personal faith or experience. Ultimately, it is a question of authority: is our reason the final judge or do we submit that reason to God?

These cautions are helpful warnings, but they are not fatal to our use of reason. God created us in his image to think, explore, discover and reason. Even without faith in God, it is possible to discover truths and make sense of aspects of our world. It is on this assumption that the next approach makes its case.

The evidence demands faith

Evidentialism is the name of a school of apologetics that emphasizes the persuasive value of evidence, regardless of whether or not one believes in God. Historically, this approach is associated with the very important work of Thomas Aquinas and, in more recent evangelical thought, with B. B. Warfield. Sometimes called 'classical apologists', these theologians sought to establish evidence for the existence of God as a first step or a foundation in an apologetic that would then be able to go on to prove the inspiration of Scripture and authority of Christ. B. B. Warfield sets out the apologetic procedure as: 'first establish Theism, then the historical credibility of the Scriptures, and then the divine origin of Christianity'.[7]

Another example of an evidentialist would be Joseph Butler (1692–1752),[8] who used examples from nature, such as the findings of biologists, as positive evidences for the truth of Christianity and as stepping stones for evangelism. Everyone can agree on the discoveries and observations of scientists, and therefore everyone ought to agree on reasonable inferences. A reasonable inference from the evidence of design and complexity in nature, according to Butler, is the existence of a divine Creator we call God. Scientific discoveries become the basic data or evidence from which we make this inference.

Many contemporary evidentialists dwell less on general philosophical arguments for the existence of God and focus more on the specific historical arguments for the reliability of the New Testament. They do not need to argue that the Bible is without error or divinely inspired, though they may well believe these things, but only need argue for the fundamental reliability of the accounts of Jesus. On this basis the case for his divinity can be made. This approach has the great strength of focusing more immediately on the person of Jesus than on more general matters relating to the existence of God.

Gary Habermas defends this approach as one that uses minimal facts to make the case for faith. These minimal facts are those that both believer and non-believer can generally agree upon, and yet they provide reason to believe. Habermas offers particularly helpful arguments for the resurrection of Jesus following this method: 'Even most sceptical scholars admit a minimal core of fact pertaining to Jesus' death and the following events . . . Virtually no one doubts Jesus' death by crucifixion.'[9] These evidences are generally neutral in the sense that any reputable scholar can agree with them, regardless of their own religious outlook.

The evidentialist approach provides a relatively straightforward method for evangelism. We do not need to get bogged down in a discussion of worldviews and philosophy, but can marshal the facts and let them speak for themselves:

Rather than necessarily having to make an additional, separate move by proving God's existence before moving to the claims of Jesus when time is often at a premium, evidentialism specializes in the one-step approach, arriving at a more direct presentation of the gospel by using data that are still very persuasive.[10]

Christians can present evidences that are compelling, regardless of whether or not their non-Christian friend believes in God. Josh McDowell has done a great service to the church by compiling data to be used in just this way: 'Christianity appeals to history. It appeals to facts of history that are clearly recognizable and accessible by everyone.'[11]

Evidentialists often stress the imagery of the law court, and indeed some of their most capable apologists such as John Warwick Montgomery are trained in law. This legal framework means that evidence is being weighed up only in terms of probabilities. To be fair, the evidence cannot actually prove a conclusion. The weight of evidence only makes a conclusion probable. But apologetics can show that belief in Jesus as the Saviour who rose from the dead is more probably true than not. So evidentialism does not attempt to prove something as absolutely certain, but makes the case that Christian beliefs are more likely true than not. For example, it is more probable than not that the Bible is reliable, that Jesus worked miracles, that evil does not disprove the existence of God. Evidentialists readily admit that certainty cannot be reached through apologetics but only through the personal assurance that arises with faith. Achieving certainty is outside the remit of apologetics. So the apologist makes it his or her more limited aim to show that Christianity is more likely true than not. Indeed, in most matters of fact we have less than absolute certainty. We deal in probabilities all the time, and our view of the world around us is based on what is more likely than not.

On the face of it, this method might seem the most straight-forward way to commend Christianity. Evidentialism starts where people are, regardless of their interest in the Christian faith. It can identify points of contact and build a case for faith upon them. However, critics of evidentialism point out a number of problems.

From a Christian point of view, does it give too much credit to the power and integrity of the human mind? The reality is that the non-Christian may have deep reasons for wanting to avoid being taken where the evidence leads. The fallen human mind is sinful and self-deceptive. This is particularly difficult when we talk in terms of probabilities. Exactly how do we calculate when something is more likely than not? David Hume, an eighteenth-century critic of Christianity, argued that a miracle is always less likely than alternative explan-ations – for example, the observers were mistaken or they told deliberate lies. So for someone like Hume, a miracle is always improbable.

Critics of evidentialism also point out that it can ignore the role of worldviews and the way in which everyone makes certain assumptions about reality. Evidentialists give the impression of offering a neutral, objective argument for the Christian faith, but do they not already assume certain beliefs? Even their way of reasoning and their criteria for truth will involve complex, often undeclared, faith com-mitments. Alasdair MacIntyre has raised this important question:

> So rationality itself, whether theoretical or practical, is a concept with a history; indeed, since there are a diversity of traditions of enquiry, with histories, there are, so it will turn out, rationalities rather than rationality, just as it will also turn out that there are justices rather than justice.[12]

MacIntyre reflects on the way in which reasons and ethics are debated and discovered within what he calls 'traditions of enquiry'. We already have our stories and ways of thinking that make some conclusions plausible and others highly unlikely. MacIntyre is particularly critical of the way the modern, secular, Western world assumes that certain ways of thinking or behaving are universal, when in fact they are often quite local and particular. This is an important problem for cross-cultural mission where Christians take the gospel to cultures which don't have any long history of Christian influence. In these settings non-Christians may not share the same view of what counts as logical, reasonable or plausible.

Evidentialism works well when believer and non-believer share important common commitments. They may share a conviction that historical claims are testable and that matters of history are of importance. They may share convictions about the importance of logical precision and careful reasoning. But the wider the gap between believer and non-believer on these matters, the less compelling evidentialism will be. People are not a blank canvas when we are in conversation with them. They already have assumptions, presuppositions and traditions that shape the way they think. What may seem very plausible to us may seem highly unlikely to them.

There is a further approach to apologetics that identifies this problem and deals with it by considering the role of presuppositions.

Reformed apologetics

There are important alternatives to evidentialism that highlight the Reformation emphasis on the fall of humanity and its impact on the way we think. One important example is Reformed epistemology.

Epistemology means a theory of knowledge, and so this approach reflects on how we know things in the light of Reformed theology. Nicholas Wolterstorff outlines the case in his helpfully titled *Reason Within the Bounds of Religion*.[13] He points out that commitment to Christ should be primary in the life of a Christian, whether scholar or not. As such, that commitment to Christ will function as a basic belief: 'Since his fundamental commitment to following Christ ought to be decisively ultimate in his life, the rest of his life ought to be brought into harmony with it.'[14] All reasoning will therefore be brought into line with this basic commitment to Christ. To try to prove God exists would be like trying to prove the length of a metre or the volume of a gallon. The measure provides the basic standard or rule by which everything else is measured.

Alvin Plantinga has developed insights in common with this approach. Plantinga is probably the most significant and respected evangelical philosopher of the twentieth century. His work is influential inside both church and academia, and we will encounter him again when we address the problem of evil. Plantinga observes that there are different ways in which we come to believe things. Some beliefs arise because of reasons and evidences. Others are things we know directly: basic beliefs and not the result of some long-winded process of reasoning. Plantinga says that belief in God should be classed as this kind of direct knowledge, a basic belief. An obvious objection to this claim is that it is special pleading or even begging the question. It makes a case for belief in God that avoids the whole issue of offering proofs. Plantinga addresses this by his wider claim that actually many of the beliefs we have are basic beliefs. In particular, our belief that other people have their own minds and consciousness and experience pain like we do is a basic belief. Plantinga says,

Belief in the existence of God is in the same boat as belief in other minds, the past, and perceptual objects; in each case God has so constructed us that in the right circumstances we form the belief in question.[15]

Reformed epistemology sounds like fideism. But this is not quite fair, because according to Reformed epistemologists it is not just Christians who have faith. Everyone has faith in something. To be an atheist is still to exercise faith. The atheist, no less than the Christian, has faith in many common-sense beliefs about everyday life. As Christians we include in the latter our faith in God.

Plantinga's suggestions are plausible as a description of why the Christian may be confident, but many people do not consider them useful for apologetics. It is true that faith often does justify itself. We are entitled to believe in God on the basis of our experience of him. An elderly believer who has had faith in God all her life but has never considered the evidence or the objections may still have a real and deep faith. However, this does not help the outsider. Those who have no faith or who question faith need to see the reasons why they might themselves come to faith in God. William Lane Craig makes a helpful distinction between *knowing* something is true and *showing* something is true.[16] Plantinga is correct in his description of how we know something important is true – we know directly even if we cannot give reasons. But Plantinga's description is of little value in *showing* something is true – by giving reasons or evidences to those who do not believe. The best Reformed apologists offer responses to objections to Christianity but provide few reasons to commend Christianity to the non-believer. For example, Plantinga has provided a highly influential response to the objection that suffering counts against the existence of the Christian God.

However, he is less confident of the value of apologetics positively to provide reasons for belief in God.

Presuppositionalism is the formal name of a tradition of apologetics that has become highly influential among evangelicals. The insights of this particular stream are not exclusive to it, but echo the thoughts of many who are critical of classical apologetics. We can find examples of apologists who tended towards this position all through the ages, but it is particularly associated with the theologians of the Reformation.

Cornelius Van Til (1895–1987) was a professor of apologetics at Westminster Theological Seminary. He dismissed evidential apologetics as an attempt to find neutral common ground between believer and non-believer. In contrast, he claimed that one must presuppose the truth of the Bible as the Word of God if one is to have any true knowledge at all. Therefore, the task of apologetics is to demonstrate the futility of all non-Christian thought. Without the Word of God, we have no basis for our use of logic, reason or moral values. The non-Christian is futile in his thinking. The basic presupposition of the Christian faith, that the Bible is God's revealed Word, provides a foundation for all knowledge.

Van Til was critical of the evidential approach in only ever being able to provide probable arguments for faith. For example, according to evidentialists, the historical evidence for the resurrection of Jesus may be demonstrated as more probable than any of the alternatives. However, probability falls short of proof and fails as a basis for faith. By contrast, the basic presupposition of the truthfulness of God's Word can be held with self-attesting certainty. In theological language, this is the inner witness of the Spirit to the truth of God's own Word. Following his understanding of John Calvin, Van Til argued that a Reformed approach to apologetics should always start with the presupposition that the Bible is our authority.

On the basis of this method, Van Til described apologetics as the attempt to show how any alternatives to historic Christianity descend into irrationality. The apologist should demonstrate on the basis of a non-believer's own ideas how hopeless and self-refuting they are: 'He should do so self-consciously, with the purpose of showing that its most consistent application not merely leads away from Christian theism but in leading away from Christian theism leads to destruction of reason and science as well.'[17] Presuppositionalists generally follow the route of negative apologetics – presenting arguments against objections to Christianity.

Having shown how inconsistent or self-contradictory the alternatives are, the apologist can then present the coherence of Christianity. It's true that Christians presume the authority of the Word of God, but on the basis of this presupposition the whole of reality makes sense. Therefore the Christian is entitled to hold this presupposition with complete assurance. The inner witness of the Holy Spirit confirms this basic assurance. The job of the apologist is to show the greater explanatory power of the Christian faith against any rival. Christianity provides a basis for meaning, purpose, logic, history and creation. Van Til argued that any alternative belief system would fail to provide an adequate explanation for them. The non-Christian may want to be logical, but without the Word of God he has no basis for his logic.

Van Til has influenced a number of subsequent apologists, though many have modified his work. Van Til's students included Francis Schaeffer who would become one of the most influential apologists among evangelicals, and John Frame who would provide a critical reappraisal of his mentor's work.[18] Van Til would however become very critical of Schaeffer's own ideas.

It is not fair to dismiss Van Til as a fideist. He certainly did believe that we could present and debate facts about God and the Bible. His point was that we should never give ground away by pretending that these are neutral facts that everyone can agree upon. On the contrary, all facts are already God-given facts. Whenever we use one, we are already assuming the truth about a God-created universe of facts. The very concept of a fact presupposes the existence of the God of creation and truth. It is the non-Christian who is being irrational in his use of facts, not the Christian.

John Frame engages with many loose ends in Van Til's work. One objection to Van Til and presuppositionalism is its apparent circularity. Is Van Til suggesting that we must believe Christianity is true in order to know what we mean by truth? Doesn't that commit the fallacy of being a circular argument or begging the question? How true is this method when we consider anyone's actual conversion? Some of our views changed when we became a Christian, it is true, but not all of them. Some beliefs we knew before we became Christians, and we still hold them to be true after our conversion. One reading of Van Til might imply that this is impossible. Only on the presupposition of the Bible being the Word of God can our reason be renewed and we be led to the knowledge of God. It is true that this is a circular argument, but Frame points out that this is not a fatal objection to what Van Til was proposing.

I need to make two very important clarifications. The first is that a presupposition is not the same as an assumption. It is not a hidden, first step in an argument as an assumption can be. What Van Til meant as a presupposition was the ultimate criterion for truth and meaning. It is not hidden but should

CHRISTIAN PERSUADERS | 61

be fully on display. It is not necessarily a first step. Someone may reach the presupposition that the Bible is the Word of God only after a lengthy period of criticism and reflection. A presupposition is therefore primary not in the chronological sense of being the first thing someone must believe, but in the transcendent sense of being the ultimate standard for truth.

The second clarification concerns circular arguments. Frame distinguishes between a 'vicious' circle and a 'spiral' circular argument. A vicious circle would be found in an argument of the form: 'The Bible is the Word of God because we find many scriptures which tell us that it is a record of God speaking.' This argument is true, but is less than helpful in apologetics because anyone who denies the presupposition will find it laughable. In contrast to a vicious circle, a spiral argument recognizes that upon the presupposition of God's Word one can take into account many different avenues of thought and possible data. We can go around and around different subjects, demonstrating the coherence of the Bible and the irrationality of the alternatives.

> If we reach an impasse over the issue of authority, we can talk about something else – history, science, psychology, or whatever. In doing so, the Christian will not abandon biblical authority, but will apply biblical authority to matters outside the Bible. And he will challenge the unbeliever so to apply his ultimate criteria.[19]

We should not use evidences as if they were neutral data upon which the Christian and non-Christian can agree. Much more emphasis should be placed on critiquing the worldview of the non-Christian. The non-Christian is not simply mistaken about a few facts here and there, such as the resurrection of Jesus or proofs for his divinity. The non-Christian is profoundly mistaken in the very basis of her outlook on life, the universe and everything else. What he or she needs is not evidences but complete conversion or regeneration of the mind. If the non-Christian does agree with the Christian on some historical observation or logical step, then it is more a testament to her inconsistency than a compliment to her rationality. That inconsistency should be teased out to demonstrate her need for a new presupposition. Traditional evidential apologetics is in danger of paying a compliment to her inconsistent rationality and only serving to encourage arrogant commitment to reason.

Presuppositionalists are very sceptical of traditional arguments for the existence of God. At best, such arguments demonstrate the existence of a 'designer' of the universe or an 'unmoved mover'. But such beings are much less than the God of the Bible and therefore as much idols as any god of paganism. Van Til asserts, 'No one can become a theist unless he becomes a Christian. Any god that is not the Father of our Lord Jesus Christ is not God but an idol.'[20] We might as well be trying to prove the existence of Baal. Instead, presuppositionalists start with a biblically informed view of God as the personal, eternal, trinitarian Creator and argue that the universe cannot be understood other than in the light of his existence. They claim this is a more honest approach to apologetics than the apparent neutrality of classical or evidential apologetics.

Conclusion

We see how Christians have sought to explain their method for apologetics. Fideism comes in many forms, but is generally sceptical of the role of rational arguments for faith. Evidentialism builds the case for faith on the basis of facts available

to everyone from history, science and experience. Presuppositionalism denies that we can start with neutral facts. We must
all have certain ultimate commitments by which we will
measure all claims to truth. For the Christian this must be
something like the Bible being the Word of God or Jesus
Christ being Lord.

This is an overview of the various perspectives that have
been offered for apologetics. Some Christians believe we must
choose between them and that they represent mutually
exclusive options. In the next chapter we will review this claim
and consider the work of apologists who cannot be labelled
so neatly.

4. For the sake of argument

No doctrine of that Faith seems to me so spectral, so unreal as the one that I have just successfully defended in a public debate.[1]
C. S. Lewis

The three broad categories we have just surveyed are often in conflict with one another. Theologians clearly debate the right approach to apologetics. So, as if our task in reaching a sceptical world is not already hard enough, we may also have to mount a defence with other Christians for what we are doing.

Cornelius Van Til was critical of evidentialism for offering only a probable argument for the existence of God. In effect, he pointed out that the evidentialists are conceding too much ground to the non-believer. They are accepting the non-believers' approach to reason and belief. This is often shown in practice. The evidentialist uses only evidences that a non-Christian would also accept in order then to demonstrate reasons for believing in God. The presuppositionalist is opposed to this method because it is the intellectual equivalent of a Trojan Horse. The evidentialist has accepted a set of non-Christian presuppositions in order to make his case for faith. The Trojan Horse of non-Christian rationality has been brought in, and from it will emerge all kinds of anti-Christian implications. For example, if we use the evidences of contemporary science for the existence of God, then we have given authority to secular scientists who may also provide reasons to dismiss faith in God.

On the other hand, the presuppositionalist can be criticized for not recognizing what is sometimes called 'natural theology'. Natural theology builds on the fact that God has endowed all people with knowledge that helps them live in a God-created world. Even without knowledge of Scripture or Christ, the non-Christian can make valid discoveries and valid arguments. The Christian is betraying nothing by using such natural arguments and evidences to demonstrate the truth of the Christian faith.

The fideist tends to criticize all these approaches for giving too much credence to the human mind, whether regenerate or not. Conversion is the result of a work of the Holy Spirit, not the conclusion of a logical argument. Therefore, while we may present our faith in many different ways, we have no alternative but to preach the gospel and pray for conversion if we want to see someone come to faith in God. Arguments and evidences are all beside the point.

Choosing an approach

Do we really have to choose between these positions? Certainly, at their core these methods are mutually exclusive, and Christians squabble among themselves over their value. They offer contrasting approaches to evangelism and often have quite different theological priorities. Evidentialists take an optimistic view of reason and human nature. Presuppositionalists generally take a stronger view of the influence of sin on the way we think. Fideists lay stress on the work of the

Spirit and hold a low view of human intellectual endeavour as far as the things of God are concerned.

But all three approaches have something to say, and in many ways most Christians will draw upon something of each. In particular, our method of apologetics will often depend on our context. If we are sharing our faith with someone from a nominally Christian background, we may well use arguments that sound evidentialist. We share enough ideas about reason and history for us to provide evidences, without worrying too much about esoteric questions such as why we believe history matters or how logic works. If pushed, any evidentialist will ultimately attribute the value of logic and history to the God who created all these things. But in the course of a debate there is no need to raise this foundational question. However, if we are sharing our faith with someone who has not grown up with that Christian background or who has rejected it in favour of some radical postmodern stance, then evidentialism will not work so well. They may have a quite different approach to reason, logic and the value of history. With such friends, we may do well to admit our presuppositions and focus more on the incoherence of any worldview that does not have the God of the Bible as a basic presupposition. Apologetics is a flexible discipline because it is a response to questions and objections. It depends on what those questions are and who is asking the questions.

Know your audience

Apologetics will also vary according to the experiences and interests of the Christian. Personalities and training are inevitably reflected in one's attitude to evangelism. In a perceptive comment, Boa and Bowman observe: 'It is no accident that evangelical scientists tend to be evidentialists or that evangelical artists tend to be fideists.'[2]

Scientists use a methodology that emphasizes the testing of hypotheses with the data of observations. This lends itself to an evidentialist approach to testing Christian truth claims. Artists tend to emphasize more creative approaches to understanding the soul or meaning of life. The emphasis is more upon feeling and convictions than observational data. Of course, there is no reason to force anyone to choose between these alternatives. Both elements of evidentialism and fideism can inform the same apologetic for Christianity. It is important to be true to the kind of people God has made us. If we are not personally persuaded of a case for Christianity, then it is likely to sound dull or unconvincing to others.

Knowing our audience is crucial for apologetics just as it is for evangelism. Our real aim is to present the claims of Christ in a way that is winsome and intelligible. We do not want to distort claims or use underhand reasoning. But we do want to engage with our friends where they are at. For this reason, it may be that the question of method is partly pragmatic. How can we best communicate our faith to this friend or this group of people in particular? Evangelism among students can highlight this challenge. One moment we are talking to someone with a nominal, traditional Christian background, but the next moment it is someone brought up in a Buddhist culture. This pluralist environment can be disconcerting. There is no one method or approach that will suit all. In some respects our context is not dissimilar to that of the early church.

Consider the example of Paul who is described as an apostle to the Gentiles. When communicating to fellow Jews, it is not surprising that Peter and Paul both appealed primarily to the teachings of Scripture. Their audience assumed the trustworthiness of the Hebrew Scriptures, and if they could persuade their hearers that what they were teaching was taught by the Scriptures, then their case was made. The apostles describe the life, death and resurrection of Jesus as the fulfilment of what the Scriptures had said. Peter explains the events of Pentecost as the fulfilment of Scripture (Acts 2). In a single sermon he cites five different references from the Hebrew Bible. When Stephen has to explain his faith before the Jewish leadership, he presents a lengthy description of the history of the Old Testament story of salvation illustrated by at least nine direct Scripture references (Acts 7). The first speech of Paul recorded in Acts is a presentation of the claims of Jesus in the synagogue at Pisidian Antioch (Acts 13). The sermon includes at least five direct quotations. In the synagogue at Thessalonica, Luke describes Paul as reasoning 'from the Scriptures, explaining and proving that the Christ had to suffer and rise from the dead' (Acts 17:2–3).

However, Paul moves beyond the Jewish circles to share his faith among the Gentiles. As he does so, his messages no longer rely on direct citation from Scripture. Among the Greek pagan agricultural community of Lystra, Paul uses the evidence of creation, but makes no reference to Scripture (Acts 14:14–18). In Athens, among Greek pagan intellectuals, a lengthy speech is recorded by Luke that has no direct Scripture reference, but does cite one pagan inscription and at least two pagan poets.[3] Paul does not treat these sources as having the authority of Scripture, but he uses them as points of contact for explaining his faith.

So the method of presenting the gospel depends on the context. People and the communities to which they belong have their own ideas about what is rational, plausible and important. Effective evangelism requires us to start where we can in our presentation of the gospel. Many of the most influential apologists of recent history have not subscribed neatly to one of the methods of apologetics alone.

Francis Schaeffer the apologist

Francis Schaeffer (1912–84) was one of the most significant apologists among evangelicals. Trained under Cornelius Van Til at Westminster Theological Seminary, he understood the presuppositionalist concerns. However, he also parted company from his former professor and modified this approach in a way that made it much more amenable to evidentialism.

Schaeffer produced a sweeping overview of Western thought in which he identified the decline of Christianity. Three of his works were later published as a single-volume trilogy and form a detailed statement of his apologetics. *The God Who Is There*, *Escape from Reason* and *He Is There and He Is Not Silent* describe the cultural shift that occurred during the twentieth century. Schaeffer believed that everyone had presuppositions in their thinking. No-one is neutral in their view of facts and values. But these presuppositions have undergone a seismic shift during recent history, and contemporary culture thinks quite differently from the people of a hundred years ago. This shift in thinking is marked by a line of despair. Prior to this shift, men and women in Western culture generally believed in a unified, rational system of thought. But since the shift, there is no longer an absolute basis for reason and morals. Schaeffer asked, 'Do we Christians understand this shift in the contemporary world? If we do not understand it, then we are largely talking to ourselves.'[4] With the voice of a prophet, Schaeffer saw the church of his time as losing its voice. It could not be heard because it could not be understood.

In many ways his books are not presenting a system of apologetics so much as a strategy for evangelism. Schaeffer believed that the church was a hundred years out of date in its attempt to evangelize the Western world. Christians were answering questions that were no longer being asked and assuming beliefs that were no longer being held. They needed to grasp the changing worldview of contemporary culture in order to explain the Christian faith intelligibly to the modern world. In a letter to Colin Duriez, he wrote, 'To me apologetics only had value in so far as it was related to evangelism.'[5] This is a revealing comment. There is a healthy pragmatism in Schaeffer's appropriation of apologetics for the purpose of evangelism. He went on to state, 'I don't believe there is any one apologetic that meets all the needs any more than I believe there is one form of evangelism that meets all the needs.'[6]

Schaeffer was criticized by his former teacher, Van Til, for his failure fully to adhere to presuppositional apologetics. The fact is, Schaeffer only drew from Van Til the very general outline of a biblical approach to apologetics – he did not use Van Til's specific system. Schaeffer believed we needed to identify the presuppositions of non-Christians and demonstrate their weakness. But with his evangelist heart, he also sought to build bridges to enable non-Christians to come to faith. This is a good lesson for us all in the use of apologetics. We have to listen to the world we want to reach and engage with the real objections and alternatives it offers.

C. S. Lewis the apologist

Another highly influential Christian communicator was C. S. Lewis. No-one can study apologetics without a close encounter with his varied writings. Clive Staples Lewis (1898–1963) is best remembered for his fantasy fiction set in his vivid world of Narnia. The stories themselves have great apologetic value, as they communicate aspects of Christian truth within the setting of beautiful children's stories. Lewis was an academic who specialized in medieval English literature but also had a broad interest in theology, philosophy and popular literature. His science fiction trilogy engages with a range of matters from the historic doctrine of the fall to the contemporary nature of science and progress.

Lewis became a Christian at the age of thirty-two.[7] Having been brought up with nominal religious leanings, he was essentially an atheist until his conversion, which was partly the result of long conversations with friends like J. R. R. Tolkien. Lewis's conversion was a thoughtful process that included overcoming intellectual objections to Christianity. Perhaps partly because of this process, his later writing and radio broadcasting were particularly well received by honest sceptics and the non-religious. He aimed to communicate Christian truth in a way that engaged with ordinary people and their everyday objections. That he did so with an effective style of communication is demonstrated by the enduring appeal of his apologetics to people from all backgrounds.

His most famous presentation of the case for Christianity is entitled *Mere Christianity* and was adapted from a series of radio talks. Lewis used the existence of a universal moral law as a point of contact to build his argument. He demonstrated that people of any religion or no religion at all have recognized an objective moral law. When we feel wronged by someone else, we appeal to this standard. The fact that our opinion about what is right or wrong may vary in different circumstances does not detract from our common conviction that right and wrong are still objective categories. The assumption that there can be moral progress over time also demonstrates an objective moral order which provides this ultimate standard of progress. The existence of this natural moral law points to the existence of a supernatural moral lawgiver behind it. Lewis approaches the issue by starting with ideas or values that everyone has, regardless of their view of the Bible. On the basis of this point of contact, Lewis carefully lays out the problem of sin and our need for forgiveness, followed by the remedy provided by the unique incarnation of God in Christ.

A similar approach to building the case for Christianity can be found throughout Lewis's work. He used the existence of desire to construct an argument that our longings always have some object that would provide satisfaction. We experience thirst and hunger because water and bread exist to satisfy them. Even if we personally die of starvation, the desire still pointed to an objective reality that lay beyond us. Therefore, if we have a longing that cannot be satisfied in this world, then 'the most probable explanation is that . . . we were made for another world'.[8] Likewise, Lewis used the existence of rationality to refute naturalism. If naturalism claims to be able to explain all of existence without reference to anything outside of the natural order, then how can rationality itself be explained? Lewis argued in *Miracles* that we must begin with God in order to have a basis for rationality itself.[9] This particular book had an interesting history. Part of it formed the text for a debate Lewis engaged in with Elisabeth Anscombe, a Roman Catholic philosopher, in 1948. It is generally thought that Anscombe won the debate. As a result, Lewis rewrote and strengthened his argument in the form that it appears in our contemporary editions.

Lewis rejected fideism: 'I am not asking anyone to accept Christianity if his best reasoning tells him that the weight of the evidence is against it.'[10] This is precisely why Lewis offers thoughtful evidence for believing in Christ. Once we have come to believe, faith describes the way that we hold on to our beliefs, despite uneven emotions and changing moods. But Lewis was not simply an evidentialist in his apologetics either. He engaged with the presuppositions and assumptions of modern thought, showing how they failed to make sense on their own terms or were themselves crying out for a divine explanation.

The genius of Lewis becomes ever clearer when we consider the diversity of approaches that he drew upon to make the case for Christianity. Apart from *Mere Christianity* and *Miracles*, the fantasy and science fiction novels along with *The Screwtape Letters* and *Surprised by Joy* provide essential apologetic reading. Lewis was able to help the Christian think about how to share his faith and engage directly with the non-Christian reader. These are skills all Christians should strive for.

Apologetics in dialogue

David K. Clark has pointed out that the approaches we have considered all offer some value, but none gives a definitive approach to apologetics.[11] The fact is that our presentation of the gospel will vary with the audience or friend we are addressing. Clark calls this 'person-centred' apologetics. In effect, apologetics must involve dialogue. It must involve listening. We listen to hear the questions or objections that need to be addressed. We listen to identify the worldview or points of contact that we can use as starting points. We listen to understand the language and concepts most appropriate to convey the gospel in terms that will communicate. The gospel and truth of God revealed in Scripture remains immovable. But the way this is communicated and the objections to which we respond are ever-changing. This makes apologetics all the more demanding, whether we are engaging with the general culture we are part of or the unique attitudes of a close friend. Clark makes our task even harder by pointing out the roles of other factors, such as the attitude of my friend (is she prejudiced against certain words I use?) and the culture to which she belongs (how does culture colour what we think is plausible or ridiculous?). Apologetics is also person-centred because we are all different. Some of us are more creative or artistic; others are more scientific and technical. Some love nothing more than reading the latest scientific theories; others just want to play and talk football. These traits will feed into the way we share our faith, and apologetics is no worse for having varied styles among believers.

To grasp the changing forms of apologetics, we need to understand how culture has altered. The constantly shifting ideas and values of Western culture have forced Christians to keep on their toes if they are to communicate clearly and effectively. We now turn to explore the historical development of apologetics.

5. Apologetics through the ages

If you would understand anything, observe its beginning and its development.
Aristotle

Where did it begin?

If we are to engage with culture, then we obviously need to ask why people think the way they do. A missionary heading into a nation which has had very little Christian influence will prepare by studying the worldview of that nation. Schaeffer and Lewis were both, in their own ways, missionaries.

Philosophy is highly influential on a culture. Ideas have legs. Ideas set in motion the capabilities of men and women to create works of art, go to war and build spaceships. It was an idea that motivated Christopher Columbus to set sail. Karl Marx had an idea that changed the face of Eastern Europe. Ideas have ruined empires and produced beauty. As Viktor Frankl, the holocaust survivor, commented, 'The gas chambers of Auschwitz, Treblinka, and Maidanek were ultimately prepared not in some Ministry or other in Berlin, but rather at the desks and in the lecture halls of nihilistic scientists and philosophers.'[1] Therefore, Christian witness must respond not only to the apparent needs or issues in culture, but to the underlying ideas and ways of thinking that inform culture. This is an area where Christians can be weak. We may be strong in practical social action or church management, but weak in responding to the philosophy of our age.

The New Testament itself provides a clear example of confident Christian engagement with the ideas of the time. John's Gospel and letters are considered by many to be a response to an early misunderstanding of Jesus that accepted his spiritual significance, but found his incarnation as a real person of flesh and blood distasteful. This misunderstanding would develop into an important heresy called Gnosticism. John describes the litmus test of a true spirit: 'Every spirit that acknowledges that Jesus Christ has come in the flesh is from God' (1 John 4:2). This seems a very precise and narrow test for the bewildering range of claims made about Jesus in our own times, but at the time of John this was a pressing issue – was Christ really incarnate in human flesh? Luke's Gospel is a deliberate attempt to provide an orderly account of history, probably in a way accessible to a non-Jewish audience (Luke 1:1–4). Paul writes Galatians in response to a legalistic distortion of the gospel (Galatians 1:6). The New Testament is not written as a collection of poetic reflections on the life of Jesus, but as a presentation of the case for Christ in response to a sceptical or confused culture. The New Testament is Christian apologetics.

The heart of the apologetic of the New Testament is that Jesus Christ had been raised from the dead and that this fulfilled the Hebrew Scriptures. The New Testament pre-supposed a familiarity and respect for the Jewish Scriptures. The most significant development in Christian apologetics is hinted at by Paul's speech to the Athenians (Acts 17). The early church had to engage a non-Jewish world in the defence and proclamation of the faith, and Paul was a trailblazer in showing the way to take on paganism.

Before we go any further, it is worth considering the influential ideas of classical Greek philosophy. It was into this culture that the first Christian apologists had to present the gospel.

It's all Greek to me

Three great Greek philosophers have had a lasting effect on Western thought: Socrates (469–399 BC), Plato (427–347 BC) and Aristotle (384–322 BC). The work of Socrates is only really known to us through the recollections of his disciple Plato. From earliest times, Christian thinkers had borrowed the ideas of Plato to try to understand their own faith.

Plato believed in a 'metaphysical' realm. Metaphysical simply means 'beyond the physical' and describes anything beyond the reach of normal sense experience. The physical world around us is a world of things we can see, touch and explore. However, thought gives us access to a world beyond. Plato used the illustration of a 'cave' to describe the difference between these two realms.

It is as if we are prisoners living deep in a cave, with a fire behind us that lights up the cave walls. Chained to the floor, we only sit and watch the shadows that play across the rocky surface. The shadows may be our own or shadows cast by other objects moved around behind us. We give words to the things we see and imagine that this is reality. But of course, all we see are the shadows – not the realities themselves. Like the prisoners, most people think that the world of shadows is all that there is. However, on reflection, the philosopher discerns the existence of the fire and the source of light.

Through the mind, we are able to loose the chains and grasp the real, perfect forms and begin to understand the true nature of reality. The original *Matrix* film by the Wachowski brothers echoed some of this thinking, as its lead character Neo grasps that the reality he had thought was true turns out to be only a virtual reality projected by alien forces.

Thought is a powerful thing, and the careful use of reason will bring us to higher and more eternal truths than our normal senses would reveal. Among these truths lies the existence of some kind of God. Plato's confidence that the natural order around us is only explained by the existence of a Supreme Creative Intellect led many early Christians to see Plato as a pagan saint. Though he lived far from the Israelite people of God with their special revelation, he had somehow come to grasp the existence of a God not dissimilar to theirs. This high regard for Plato led to his philosophy having a great influence on many of the early Christian theologians. Some even earned the nickname 'neo-Platonists' for their attempt to synthesize Plato and the Bible. Augustine (AD 354–430) is regarded by many as one of the most influential early Christian theologians to have borrowed from Plato. One of the first Christians to write specific apologetic works in the early church was Justin Martyr (AD 100–165) who was converted from a background in Platonic philosophy. Rather than reject Platonism altogether, he sought to blend these ideas with his Christian faith.

If ideas have legs, then Plato's ideas have been on a marathon. Some of his influences on Christian theology have not always been welcome. The distinction between the spiritual and the physical would come to detract from the Hebrew worldview with its emphasis on the spirituality of ordinary life. Some Christians have blamed the dualism of flesh and spirit on Plato's legacy. This dualism has downgraded sex and manual labour to something less spiritual than contemplation and religious rituals. If we imagine the spirit is an immaterial soul trapped in the physical body, then we are likely to devalue physical activities. This contrasts with the Hebrew worldview of the Bible where worship involves ordinary daily living and the things of God being taught around the family meal table. A Platonic devaluing of nature has been blamed for the way Christian theology may have neglected the importance of creation and care for the environment.

Aristotle would also prove to be highly influential on Christian apologetics in the later Middle Ages, but first let us consider the early church.

The early church

Fragments of the very earliest Christian writings from the second century are clear examples of apologetics. Justin Martyr was one of the most formidable early Christian apologists. All his surviving works are examples of apologetics, including a dialogue with a Jewish rabbi.

Much of what Justin wrote was a defence of Christian loyalty to the Roman Empire. However, he also engaged with objections to the Christian faith from pagan philosophy and Jewish theology. Justin provides a very clear defence of the physical resurrection of Jesus from the dead. He refutes any notion of a spiritual resurrection or an immaterial appearance of Jesus (a misunderstanding very much back in vogue in our own times). Regarding pagan philosophy, he used the idea of the *logos* (word) to form a bridge with non-Christians. Wherever truth could be found among non-Christians Justin identified the work of the Divine Logos. This partial work of the Logos bringing light among the pagans was brought to completion in the incarnation of Jesus Christ. In this way,

Justin was able to write a positive appreciation of Socrates, the early Greek philosopher, in whom the Logos had been at work. His positive treatment of the Greeks included the argument that Plato had read and borrowed from the Old Testament.[2] His dialogue with the Jewish rabbi is both friendly and challenging – an example which would rarely be copied in years to come.

Sadly, many of the early apologists were more sympathetic to Greek philosophical thought than to Jewish rabbinical teaching. There tended to be a very negative evaluation of how the Jews understood the law and prophecy, while the positive value of classical Greek thinking encouraged turning a blind eye to its failings. The reality was that many of the apologists were primarily motivated by establishing the respectability of Christianity in the modern world. To do that, distancing themselves from Judaism and finding common cause with Greek philosophy may have seemed an attractive move. But it would also create problems of its own. For example, Origen (AD 185–254) dismissed some of the teachings of Moses as irrational and preferred to interpret much of the Bible as allegory. More seriously still, he drew on Greek classical thought to argue for unbiblical ideas such as the eternal existence of the soul and for the universal salvation of all souls. Origen provides a cautionary example of the apologist who allows a rational chain of thought radically to reinterpret Scripture. Apologetics is dangerous when it distorts the clear meaning of the Bible in order to make it more plausible.

Among the early apologists, a central theme was the resurrection of Jesus. Origen used evidence from history, fulfilled prophecy, and psychology to great effect. For example, in his work *Contra Celsum*, he argued that the disciples would not have invented the resurrection of Jesus because they would not have been willing to suffer and die for a lie. Nor would it be the product of hallucination because the resurrection was observed by reasonable people in ordinary circumstances. These examples show that Origen was concerned for a historical, physical resurrection and gave reasons for it.

One of the most important apologists among the early Christians was Eusebius (AD 263–339). His importance is measured not so much by his original contribution to the defence of the faith, but rather by his influence on the theology that followed him. Eusebius became an advisor to Emperor Constantine, the first Roman emperor officially to endorse Christianity. As he held such a position of influence, certain themes in his apologetics bear highlighting. Eusebius wrote extensively in defence of Christianity. He was particularly interested in the historical credentials of the New Testament, which was reflected in his concern for the faithful preservation of the text – he had fifty copies of the Bible made. Christians and Jews have always been people of the book, concerned for the faithful transmission of their texts.

Eusebius defended the universality of the Christian faith – an important theme if it was to become the official religion of the Roman Empire. To do so he discredited the paganism of classical Greece and the law of Moses as both temporary and local forms of religion. Instead, he found universal codes in the Patriarchs (Abraham, Isaac and Jacob) with their simple monotheism, and in Greek philosophy. Like many before him, Eusebius seemed more comfortable with Greek philosophy than with the Hebrew Bible.

Augustine the apologist

No survey of early-church theology, ministry or apologetics can ignore the impact of Augustine (AD 354–430). Converted from a pagan background, he had known the lure of the world but became a passionate defender of the Christian faith. His wide range of writings is peppered with reasonable arguments. Augustine was also influenced by the work of the classical Greek philosopher Plato, mentioned above.[3] The distinction between our world of illusions and the spiritual realm of absolute truth and beauty provided a fertile bridge between the New Testament and Greek philosophy. In fact, Augustine even claimed that, had Socrates and Plato lived in his day, then they would have become Christians. Platonism held to the pre-existence of the soul and a dualism of soul (what I am) and body (where my soul resides). These ideas are alien to the Hebrew worldview, but assumed by many believers brought up in the world of Greek philosophy. In one of his final works, called *Retractions*, Augustine came to acknowledge and repudiate some of Plato's ideas that had misled him.

Augustine recognized a complicated relationship between faith and reason. On the one hand, in a number of references he declared that we need to believe in order to understand. On the other hand, he was perfectly aware that we need to make a rational decision in order to come to faith. The balance between the two is found for Augustine in the authority of the church. This authority is itself based on miracles, including the miracle of the resurrection of Jesus and the miracle of the ongoing survival of the church. Miracles bear witness to the authority of the church, but it is this authority to which we must submit. This argument from authority becomes an important theme in later Roman Catholic apologetics, which would emphasize the authority of the church in matters of belief.

Some features of apologetics in this period of history stand out. Christians were keen to argue that the faith was not a threat to the Roman Empire. This reflected the uneasy relationship between Christians and the pagan state – Justin would in time be beheaded for his faith. Christians also sought to demonstrate the antiquity of their message by showing that it had been predicted and prepared for by the Jewish Hebrew Scriptures. Another general feature of apologetics in this period was the attempt to show that Christianity was compatible with, even a fulfilment of, classical Greek philosophical thought. This is perhaps the most troubling feature of early-church apologetics. Plato seemed to offer a bridge for the gospel, but on reflection many theologians would notice that this actually distorted the Christian message.

One further feature of apologetics at this time was that these people clearly felt that good writing was part of the apologetic task. It was not that they just happened to write well and produce admirable literature. They wrote at a time when rhetoric was part of good argument. It was not enough to write a logical case for Christ; it also had to be a well-written case for Christ. Reason and beauty together made a persuasive case. The early Church Fathers would have felt at home with the concerns of twentieth-century writers such as C. S. Lewis and Francis Schaeffer, who saw beauty, art and poetry as an integral part of Christian witness.

The proof for God's existence

One of the most interesting arguments for the existence of God was proposed by Anselm (1033–1109), who later became Archbishop of Canterbury, much to his own displeasure. A man of meditation and prayer, Anselm would have chosen to avoid the administrative and political burdens of public life. But his greatest impact would be his intellectual work and particularly his argument for the existence of God. The argument has been debated, rejected and defended for nearly a thousand years and remains strangely attractive. Anselm described God's existence as 'necessary'. By this, he meant that it was impossible for God not to exist. I don't have to exist. Nor do elephants or dandelions. That's because all these material things are 'contingent' – just like you. Contingent beings may or may not exist. But God is not one of these beings. God is 'a being than which nothing greater can be conceived'.[4] This seems uncontroversial. God is, by definition, the most perfect being possible – who or what could be wiser or more powerful than him? We can all, atheist or not, imagine such a being. But what if this God did not exist? Well, then it would follow that we could conceive a greater being: a God that did exist. But this is impossible because we have already defined God as a being who is greater than anything else we can conceive. So God, by definition, must exist in reality as well as in the imagination. To use our earlier language, God is a 'necessary' being. It is impossible for him not to exist. Reactions to Anselm's argument range from the angry dismissal that it is just a play on words (Schopenhauer called it 'a charming joke') to extensive discussion and promotion (defended in various forms by later philosophers Descartes, Leibniz and Plantinga).

An early objection to Anselm's argument used the analogy of a perfect island. If we substitute the word 'island' for 'God' in the argument, then we seem to be pressed to believe that there must be a perfect island somewhere in existence. This makes the argument seem silly. However, defenders have argued that the island example does not work because it is only of God that we can really apply the attributes of complete perfection. No island necessarily exists. In fact, only of God can we say he must necessarily exist. All analogies fail because they deal with contingent objects. God is the only being of whom it can be said nothing greater can be imagined.

The ontological argument can sound strained to modern ears, but it has remained an influential one. It has routinely been rejected as an example of begging the question, but defenders like Plantinga point to its intuitive appeal. Could it be that our very ability to conceive of God presupposes his existence? However, Anselm's argument depends less on the biblical worldview than on Plato. The idea that God's existence can somehow be demonstrated on the basis of the nature of being is a very Platonic approach to truth. This helps to explain why the argument can seem so contrived to contemporary ears. As theologian Michael Reeves points out, 'The whole edifice is built upon a concealed Platonic presupposition, and Plato's time as the most influential philosopher was almost over.'[5] But in the wake of Plato, another classical philosopher was to come to dominate Western thought.

Undoubting Thomas

If Plato was a key influence on apologists in the early church, then Aristotle was the greater influence in the Middle Ages. Like Plato, Aristotle also believed that clear, logical thinking could yield truths, but he also thought that we could learn spiritual truths from studying the physical, natural world. Bertrand Russell dryly summarized Aristotle's thought as 'Plato diluted by common sense'.[6] Aristotle saw great value in practical, scientific observation and study. Aristotle was a pioneer of science in the way we understand it in the modern world.

Aristotle's thought was taken up first by Muslim theologians and then by the Christian, Thomas Aquinas (1225–74). Though Thomas had few followers in his day, his work inspired a great following, later known as Thomism. The dependence on Aristotle gave rise to a very positive appreciation of natural logic and science. Revelation was seen as adding to knowledge already attainable through the mind. Rational thinking could establish the truth of many Christian doctrines, without requiring constant quoting of the Bible. In this way, Thomas had a high regard for philosophy as a method distinct from theology and the Bible. The philosophy of Greek thinkers like Aristotle provides useful steps for coming to a knowledge of God: 'Accordingly, divine wisdom sometimes argues from principles of human philosophy.'[7] Indeed, one of Thomas's most influential works, the *Summa Contra Gentiles*, is a work of apologetics aimed especially at missionaries working among Muslims, and is heavily reliant on Aristotle. Thomist thought, as it became known, placed great emphasis on these possibilities of natural knowledge. Genuine knowledge of God and his world can be had through the careful use of rational thought.

The thought of Thomas Aquinas became a standard for theology within the Roman Catholic Church. The great legacy of Thomas is the high regard within Catholicism for natural theology. Through to modern times, his influence has been felt in the work of key Catholic theologians Hans Küng and Karl Rahner. Thomas also had his followers among evangelicals, and he offers some powerful ideas for apologetics. His most famous example is the 'five ways' in which we can prove the existence of God.

Does God's existence need proof? In one sense, Thomas says no. God's existence is more certain than the existence of creation itself. In another sense, Thomas says yes. For to our limited, weak minds, the creation seems an awful lot more real than spiritual things. So the existence of God 'needs to be made evident by means of things less evident in themselves but more evident to us, namely God's effects.'[8] Each of the five ways reasons from things we do know or see to the conclusion that God must exist.

The five ways sound similar to our ears. They all emphasize that the things we see around us are effects needing an explanation. The ultimate or final explanation in each case is God. Motion is ultimately explained by an unmoved mover (the first way). Causes are explained by a first cause (the second way). The apparent design of creation is explained by a designer (the fifth way). But, someone might object, why should there be an ultimate explanation? Why can't a chain of cause and effect go back infinitely? This possibility is rejected as irrational because of the problem of an 'infinite regress'.[9] Some of Thomas's arguments remain popular in apologetics to this day. For example, the argument from a first cause works particularly well with the Big Bang as an established scientific hypothesis. What caused the Big Bang? Thomas Aquinas would have had a ready answer.

What is also worth noticing about the five ways is that Thomas borrows all of them from Aristotle. He is aware that this raises an interesting point. Without the Bible or faith in Christ, it is possible to use our natural reason to work out many important things about God. This seems a great strategy for apologetics. It also suggests that we should hold the pagan philosophers in high esteem. God has implanted reason within each one of us, and using it can lead us to knowledge of God – even without the Bible. So just as Anselm's ontological argument made more sense in a world influenced by Plato, Thomas's ideas have more appeal to a world indebted to Aristotle.

The Reformation

The Middle Ages were followed by a period called the Renaissance. From around the fourteenth century, the re-discovery of the Greek philosophers was accompanied by a flowering of art, literature and science. Because people wanted to get back to the sources of these great ideas, Greek flourished as a language, whereas for many centuries it had been eclipsed by Latin. Alongside the Greek philosophers, other Greek documents started to be read again. For centuries, the New Testament of the Bible had only really been studied in Latin. When a Roman Catholic called Erasmus began to study the sources for the Latin New Testament, he began to discover that there were significant distortions of the original Greek. Rediscovering the original sources for biblical teachings was a significant factor in the Reformation. Behind the many layers of Roman Catholic tradition and Latin writings lay the simple faith of the Greek New Testament. The approach to reason and natural theology that had bogged down the Middle Ages fell on hard times. The great figures of the Reformation had little time for Thomas Aquinas or any of the Greek philosophers.

Martin Luther (1483–1546) was scathing in his condemnation of natural reason. He dismissed natural theology and denied that reason could lead to faith. However, Luther was not dismissing reason in general. His fiery rhetoric was aimed at the kind of rational theology that had suppressed true faith. In his own work he could employ reasonable arguments, and in apologetics engage in communicating the faith to nonbelievers. Luther wrote extensively on Islam, demonstrating an interest in Islamic teaching, if only in order to refute it.

John Calvin (1509–64) did not engage with classical philosophers in the way that Thomas Aquinas had done. However, he did believe that some natural sense of God and morality was to be found in all people, though only the Bible and inner work of the Spirit brought about personal faith. Many Christian apologists look to Calvin as their exemplar. Calvin, like Luther, was not writing directly on the subject of apologetics, and so we must read between the lines of what he had to say. His systematic theology, particularly *The Institutes of the Christian Religion*, does provide clear guidelines for the limits of reason. Reason helps us to make sense of the Bible and creation. But reason alone does not lead us to a saving knowledge of God.

The Reformers emphasized the damage done by the fall. What Calvinists called 'total depravity' was the teaching that every aspect of human life is in some way affected by the fall. They did not mean that we are totally depraved. Their point was that depravity (sin) affects the totality of our lives. This included our use of logic and reason. This is why the Reformers were suspicious of the efforts of philosophers and natural theologians to try to prove the existence of God. This Reformation suspicion would continue into more recent times in the work of the Swiss theologian, Karl Barth.

Calvin had a place for rational arguments, but only as a limited preparation for the work of the Spirit in bringing someone to faith.

> Profane men think that religion rests only on opinion, and therefore that they may not believe foolishly, or on slight grounds, desire and insist to have it proved by reason that Moses and the prophets were divinely inspired. But I answer, that the testimony of the Spirit is superior to reason. For as God alone can properly bear witness to his own words, so these words will not obtain full credit in the hearts of men, until they are sealed by the inward testimony of the Spirit.[10]

Calvin identifies the weakness of rational arguments. First, they can only provide probable evidence, not certainty. Secondly, they assume the authority of someone other than God – either the authority of the church or the scholar. In contrast, God is his own authority and so his Word is self-attesting. Through an inward work of the Spirit, we can become convinced of the truth with a certainty that goes beyond reasons. But these weaknesses in rational arguments are not fatal. They still have their place. Calvin's own work provides a very clear example of rational, careful argument.

The Age of Enlightenment

The philosophy of René Descartes (1596–1650) is often heralded as the beginning of a new cultural shift. A French Roman Catholic philosopher, his piety is in no doubt. He has been referred to as the father of modern philosophy. He was a brilliant thinker, and like many philosophers in past centuries he applied his intellect to many areas of knowledge. Anyone interested in geometry will be familiar with 'Cartesian co-ordinates' which are named after him. Many of his ideas were classic Catholic theology, but what interests us is his method. His philosophical method was a break with the past and a first glimpse into what became known as the Enlightenment.

In an autobiographical comment, Descartes, perhaps a little wistfully, describes his youthful ambition 'to seek the true method of arriving at knowledge of everything my mind was capable of grasping'.[11] He wanted to set aside customs, trad-itions and received opinions in favour of clear, orderly, logical thought and arrive at one sure path to certainty. Well, as youthful ambitions go, that beats the dreams of many students today!

Descartes raised the question that has haunted everyone from time to time and was behind Plato's story of the cave. What if all life is a dream or an illusion? What if nothing is as it appears – perhaps being the product of an evil intelligence or some conspiracy theory? How could we ever be sure? How would you know if you are reading this book now and not just dreaming you were reading it? In the film *The Truman Show*, the lead character thinks he is living a normal life in a small town, when unknown to him he is actually just part of a grand conspiracy creating a soap opera around him. If everyone but us is in on the conspiracy, then how would we ever know?

Descartes thought about it. What if I chose to doubt everything I had ever known? There would still be one secure truth: I doubt, therefore I exist. Or, as he would rephrase the point, *cogito, ergo sum* (I think, therefore I am). Even if I doubt everything, I cannot doubt that I am doing the doubting. Therefore, my own existence is the one certain piece of knowledge. Even if everything is an illusion, and I am deceived, the one absolutely certain fact I can be confident of is that I exist, because after all I am the one doing the doubting.

On the basis of this true proposition, Descartes went on to establish a reason to believe in the reliability of the senses, the existence of an external world and even the existence of God. He could remain a good Catholic (Augustine had already produced a similar argument). But something had changed. Descartes had established a new method. Just like maths or geometry, our knowledge of God and the world could be built upon simple, certain foundations using logical thought.

The legacy of Descartes would not be found in his new basis for faith in God, but rather in the new starting point for knowledge. It was possible to reason and understand the self and the world without first believing in God. This was the real watershed of the Enlightenment Age.

Here, then, was the prototypical declaration of the modern self, established as a fully separate, self-defining entity, for whom its own rational self-awareness was absolutely primary

– doubting everything except itself, setting itself in opposition
not only to traditional authorities but to the world, as subject
against object, as a thinking, observing, measuring,
manipulating being, fully distinct from an objective God
and an external nature.[12]

Descartes would have considered himself a faithful Catholic,
and his work includes an apologetic for faith in God. But his
method departs from those who had gone before. Knowledge
proceeds by simple steps from certain foundations to more
ambiguous ideas. The thinking self is certain; God and the
angels are ambiguous.

A British thinker came to study in France from 1675 and
encountered the work of Descartes. His name was John Locke
(1632–1704), and he would go on to become an enormous
influence on political thought and education. His thinking laid
the framework for liberal democracy and would be put to
good use by the founding fathers of the United States
Constitution who quoted him approvingly.

Locke famously described the mind as like a blank sheet of
paper (*tabula rasa*). The paper is written on by the things we
experience through our senses. As time goes by and we see
and hear more, we understand things better and the sheet
begins to fill with our experiences. Everyone starts out equally
ignorant but equally capable. The path to knowledge is
through experience. The new rising movement of modern
science would be considered the most reliable way to real
knowledge – through experience and experiment.

Locke considered himself a Christian apologist. His book,
The Reasonableness of Christianity as Delivered in the Scriptures,[13]
among other writings, was an attempt to establish the truth
of Christianity as a faith both historically grounded and
universally significant. However, critics of Locke point out

that he defends a minimalist faith which does not affirm incarnation or atonement. This would become a theme in the development of theology during the Enlightenment. Most thinkers wanted to defend Christianity, but they did so by stripping it of the content that did not fit so well with the new worldview.

The best example of this is found in perhaps the most influential Enlightenment thinker of all, Immanuel Kant (1724–1804). Born in Königsberg, Prussia, Kant never ventured out of the region of his birth. Kant was so much a man of routine, according to a famous anecdote, that the locals would set their clocks by him as he passed by on his daily walk. Kant is important for bringing together many of the new ideas of the previous century and clarifying the nature of knowledge. Even more than Descartes, Kant must be seen as a father of Enlightenment thought, because he really let go of the Catholic theology of the Middle Ages and started something new. In an essay called 'What is Enlightenment?', Kant described the previous period as a time of intellectual blindness when men and women were told what to think by the traditions of church and state. In this new era, he wrote, '*Sapere aude!* [dare to know!] "Have Courage to use your own reason" – that is the motto of enlightenment.'[14]

The rise of the modern worldview had given people a new-found confidence in reason and experience. Theology and revelation were waning in influence. But there was a significant, nagging doubt. This had been expressed by an important Scottish thinker called David Hume (1711–76), whom we have already met. He was a sceptical philosopher who wrote a popular book on religion which undermined the credibility of every important argument for the existence of God.[15] Hume assessed each argument carefully and showed how no miraculous or supernatural claim could be trusted.

His criticisms of religion remain popular to this day. However, Hume's scepticism was more radical than this single volume might suggest. He also pointed out that many of the basic things we assume about existence are strictly beyond proof. There is really no experience that we can trust. All perception is deceptive, and even Descartes' claim: 'I think, therefore I am' is far from certain. What do we mean by 'I'? Surely, all Descartes could really have concluded is: 'I think I think, therefore there are thoughts.' Hume concluded that we must humbly trust our experiences and go about our lives: 'I must yield to the current of nature, in submitting to my senses and understanding; and in this blind submission I show most perfectly my sceptical disposition and principles.'[16] Hume encouraged scepticism in all matters of knowledge, but submission to the way things appear as a practical solution for day-to-day living.

Kant described Hume as 'waking' him from his 'dogmatic slumbers'. Hume's scepticism prompted Kant to rethink the basis of knowledge. Kant accepted Hume's point that we don't experience the world directly, as Locke assumed, but we experience the world only as it appears to us. Perception is itself the object of knowledge. This is important because we know that often experience misleads us. An optical illusion is a good example because it reminds us that our mind is very busy when we see a drawing. Our mind interprets the picture and makes sense of it for us. Then we realize that we can interpret it differently, and our mind rethinks it. In many ways we know that our perceptions can be misleading, and on closer inspection reality can be quite different from the way it first appeared. These are the problems that Descartes, Locke and Hume, among many others, had all wrestled with. Kant was able to draw upon them all and formulate a new answer.

The answer is to recognize that the mind is an active part of knowledge. We never see things directly, but only through the framework of our mind. This framework was described by Kant as a collection of categories. The categories of the mind are like the scaffolding around a building site. They help the mind to order and make sense of incoming perceptions. The categories are things like time, space and numbers. The mind does not see the world directly, but through the interpretative scaffolding of these categories.

So the mind is not a blank canvas (Locke), but a busy building site already prepared to make sense of our experiences. We never have direct access to reality but only to reality as it appears to us. This implies that there are important limits to human understanding. We cannot experience or describe things that lie beyond the framework of our mind. We are limited to the world as it appears to us, and this is the only realm in which we can really have knowledge. Anything more than this would be a kind of pseudo-science.

So what is left for Christian theology? Kant considered himself a Christian and also wrote his own apologetic for Christianity, *Religion Within the Limits of Reason Alone*. In this work, Kant considered the claims of the Christian faith in the light of his understanding of human knowledge. Given these limitations, what is left? The answer is not much. Kant concluded that there was a core of Christian faith that must be true, but much of theology deals in unnecessary and unknowable wrappings that should really be discarded. The core that remains consists of a few simple beliefs in the existence of some kind of Divine Being and a moral basis for right and wrong.

The Enlightenment period saw theologians adopting a religion stripped of the specifics of the Christian faith, such as the incarnation and the atonement. This budget version of the Christian faith would focus on a simple kernel of truth, compatible with many world religions.

The Enlightenment Age would put emphasis on scientific discovery and advancement rather than received wisdom. Religion was stripped down to something more plausible, a rational religion, and pushed more to the sidelines of knowledge.

It is interesting to note that the Age of the Enlightenment lay right at the beginning of the great missionary movement. Evangelicals rediscovered the Great Commission, and with the trade routes opening across the globe found many ways of taking the gospel to the ends of the earth. Great, pioneering missionary work opened up the lands of Africa, India, China and the Americas to the gospel. Churches were established that would soon grow in size to dwarf those of Europe. The missionaries also brought Western principles of education, medicine and technology with them. In some ways, the nineteenth century could be considered a golden age for Christian mission. But while the gospel was being preached across the globe, all was not well back in Europe.

The intellectual development of Western thought in the nineteenth century was barely touched by the Bible. Despite the enormous influence of the Reformation, evangelicals made very little contribution to the academy. Both the sciences and the humanities were far more influenced by the new insights of Enlightenment thought. For all the positive influences of Christianity on social reform and popular culture, there would be a deep antipathy towards it among intellectuals.

6. Brave new world

There's probably no God . . . but I wish there was. I've got some things I need to ask him.
Marcus Brigstocke

To understand contemporary apologetics, we need to understand the age in which we live. While the Christian message remains the same, our context has certainly changed since the time of the early church. To understand the issues facing contemporary apologetics, we need to follow the story of the last chapter a little further and establish how the Western worldview has developed since the Enlightenment.

Spirits in the material world

At its heart, Western thought became materialistic. Materialism is the view that all things can be explained in the light of the natural, physical processes we see all around us. God is unnecessary in the attempt to explain the world. It is not that God does not exist, and few upstanding Victorian intellectuals would have been atheists, but it is the case that God now has no direct relevance. In the area of biology, Charles Darwin

(1809–82) was able to describe the history of organic development without reference to any spiritual influence. The same
kind of project was to be found in psychology (Ludwig
Feuerbach), economics (Karl Marx) and ethics (John Stuart
Mill). In each discipline, an attempt was made to resolve
problems and propose methods of enquiry which did not
require any reference to God as a real being. The materialist
assumes that the universe is a closed system of cause and
effect without the intrusion of a Divine Hand. If there is a
God, then his (or its) role is only to set the ball in motion, and
having done so, he has a 'hands-off' relationship with his
creation. One clear turning point in Western thought is the
publication of Darwin's *On the Origin of Species* (1859), which
probably did more than any other single book to bring the
Enlightenment revolution from the academic world to
popular culture. This can seem unlikely when anyone tries
to read the book for the first time. It is dry, measured and slow
– hardly a revolutionary tract.

The idea of evolution was not original to Darwin – his
grandfather had used the term, and alternative theories of
evolution or the transmutation of species were aleady being
proposed. Surprisingly, the word 'evolution' appears nowhere
in the text of *On the Origin of Species* (though the term
'creation' appears over a hundred times!). It was already
understood that creatures evolve or adapt over time. The
unique contribution of Darwin was his identification of a
natural law governing evolutionary change and development.
Darwin called this law 'natural selection'. Tiny variations
occur in a creature, entirely by chance: a slightly longer nose
or different colour of hair or shorter legs. Most of the time
these variations are irrelevant; often they are harmful. But
sometimes these variations help a creature to do better than
its rivals, and this will make it more likely to procreate.

Through procreation these slight variations will sometimes be passed on. So, over time, the surviving progeny will tend to be those better able to cope in the environment in which they live. This can be called 'survival of the fittest'.

The fittest creatures are not those we might judge fittest by other standards (those we deem to be bigger or more intelligent or more peaceful), but those most suited for the environment. Hence, creatures that are smaller or less complex might be better fitted for survival than more spectacular creatures. Earthworms outlasted the dinosaurs, and so the survival of the fittest favoured the humble worm.

Darwin's key contribution was to identify natural selection as the designer. Organisms may look like the product of intelligent design, but in fact are the result of a natural law governing the transmission of some variations and the erasing of others. We will come back to the issue of evolution and design in chapter 8 when we address apologetics and science, but for now it is sufficient to note that it is too simplistic to assume that Darwin's theory of evolution led to his loss of faith.[1]

Darwin expresses his views on Christianity very clearly in his autobiography. Perhaps never intended for publication, a more acceptable version for general consumption was edited by the family. However, the unexpurgated edition is very revealing. What becomes most obvious, if his autobiography is to be trusted, is that Darwin's rejection of Christianity came long before his proposal of natural selection. The grounds for his atheism were not found in the scientific theory he is remembered for, but arose from other questions he was considering.

The first question in his autobiography would become one of the most significant issues for apologetics in the modern age: How can Christianity be considered a unique way of salvation when there are so many other faiths? Since the spread of the British Empire, the Western world had become intrigued by the Eastern religions we call Hinduism and Buddhism. To claim a unique status for Christianity just seemed to reflect cultural prejudice.

The second question arises from a scepticism over miraculous claims. The modern age had come to recognize that the world was governed by natural laws. These laws of motion and energy determined how things happened. Miracles contradicted natural laws, and so for Darwin they demonstrated a pre-critical mind. That was satisfactory for earlier people who had believed in magic and superstitions, but was no longer a credible explanation of any events.

The third question Darwin raised concerned the reliability of the Gospel records themselves. In keeping with the trends of biblical studies among academics, Darwin assumed that the Gospels were inaccurate records of the life of Jesus written much later than the events they describe. Therefore, the Bible itself was not a reliable source of information.

Raising these questions eroded Darwin's faith, and 'by such reflections as these . . . [he] gradually came to disbelieve in Christianity as a divine revelation'.[2]

Then, finally, Darwin came to reject Christianity altogether because of the doctrine of everlasting punishment which he famously dismissed as 'a damnable doctrine'.[3] This is part of the problem of suffering – how can a good and all-powerful God permit suffering and pain? Darwin wrote, 'This very old argument from the existence of suffering against the existence of a first cause seems a strong one to me',[4] and the reason for suffering would find an alternative explanation in his own scientific theories.

Darwin does indicate that he remained vaguely theist until the publication of *On the Origin of Species*. His commitment to theism had been reinforced by 'the extreme difficulty, or rather impossibility of conceiving this immense and wonderful universe, including man with his capacity of looking far backwards and far into futurity, as the result of blind chance or necessity'.[5] There must be a personal God of some sort, not necessarily as conceived by Christianity, as the first cause of the universe. However, even this simple commitment to theism lost its appeal in Darwin's later years. But it is important to recognize that it was not the observations of biology that caused him to reject faith in God, but objections common to the Enlightenment Age. Christianity seemed narrow-minded, the Bible unreliable and the problem of suffering too inexplicable to make belief in God plausible. The contribution of *On the Origin of Species* was to push the need for a super-natural explanation out of the academy. If God was unnecessary to explain even the development of life itself, then quite what was the role of God?

The Christian response

This materialistic worldview dominated intellectual circles. It is not that there were no Christians involved in their various fields, for there certainly were. But their Christian convictions bore little relation to their areas of study. Christianity was a faith for the private, personal life, with no bearing on the public areas of study or discovery. Just as the great missionary movement was planting solid, lasting churches around the globe, the churches in the Western world were losing their soul. Even theology came to be dominated by a materialistic worldview. Sadly, some of these misguided movements in theology came about because of a desire to create a new, appealing apologetic in the modern age. Kant had already set the agenda: given the implausibility of miracles, revelation or incarnation, how can we be sure that there is a God?

Liberal apologetics

Kant saw faith as resting on personal moral feelings rather than on an external authority like church or the Bible. This view of faith would become very important in the years that followed. Many Christians felt that they could not defend the historical credibility of the Bible or miracles, and so conceded that faith had to be grounded on something more experiential. In effect, many apologists conceded so much ground to the materialist worldview that God was irrelevant to all the hard sciences. One of the great but misguided apologists of this period was Friedrich Schleiermacher (1768–1834). We can learn a great deal, both positive and negative, from him.

On the one hand, Schleiermacher was at odds with the new Enlightenment worldview. In fact, an entire countercultural movement was developing which we now call the Romantic Movement. This movement is associated especially with the arts, but it found theological expression in the work of Schleiermacher. What Schleiermacher found most repellent in the Enlightenment was the reduction of religion to a moral code. It made matters of faith legalistic and calculating. By contrast, along with many poets and artists, Schleiermacher wanted to emphasize the passions. Religion is not about moral codes and duty, but about an experience of God and passionate commitment. The same theme can be found throughout the Romantic Movement. Poets like Byron and Wordsworth, and artists like Caspar David Friedrich, sought to regain a sense of awe and mystery in nature and passion that was in danger of being smothered by rational thought.

But Schleiermacher did not disagree with Kant over matters of history or biblical studies. In fact, he also shared Darwin's reservations about religion. He saw the same difficulties with belief in miracles or the incarnation. But what Schleiermacher saw, and Kant missed, was the powerful experience of absolute dependence on a Divine Being that is revealed through religion. Jesus Christ, in a profound way, experienced this sense of the divine which his followers would be able to share. Therefore, the biblical record continued to retain powerful experiential value for faith, even without historical credibility.

Schleiermacher's apologetic for the Christian faith is very relevant for us, and his influence continues to be felt. No doubt he was correct to react against the loss of passionate commitment in the Christian faith. But he conceded too much in suggesting that this experience of God was independent of the value of historical revelation. He did what many Christians continue to do today when they ignore intellectual problems or questions and urge enquirers simply to seek an experience of God. Of course, many people have profound experiences, but these could lead to any number of religions or scriptures. By abandoning the reliability of the historic revelation of the Bible, there was no longer a reason to believe in the uniqueness and necessity of the Christian faith.

In theological thought, the growth of liberalism continued throughout the nineteenth century. Adolf von Harnack in *What Is Christianity?* provides a great example of the non-supernatural interpretation of Christianity. This was a highly influential set of lectures published as a book in 1900 and subsequently translated into many languages. Harnack observed that Christianity has changed in its form during the course of the centuries. Yet he remained confident that the gospel 'contains something which, under differing historical forms, is of permanent validity'.[6] What are some of the unnecessary or mistaken ideas of earlier Christians? Harnack rejects belief in the possibility of miracles since the scientific revolution: 'that a storm was quieted by a word, we do not believe, and we shall never again believe'.[7] The supernatural elements of Christianity are no more than the unnecessary packaging to be discarded in favour of the gospel message of love. Harnack was a theologian deeply influenced by the Enlightenment. Perhaps with the best of intentions, he tried to develop an apologetic for the Christian faith acceptable to his contemporaries. This became known as 'liberal Christianity'.

Some key assumptions of liberal Christianity are worth identifying. First, a new approach to reading the Bible had developed in the previous century, which came to be called Higher Criticism. This approach took a step back from reading the Bible as if the books had originally been written in the form in which we have them. Instead, it proposed that many different authors and traditions had developed over many years and been fused together by later editors. Consequently, nothing we read in the Bible can be taken at face value. Lying behind this approach was an evolutionary view of human knowledge (not to be confused with biological evolution). For many years prior to Darwin, scholars had assumed that human culture had evolved from the simple and primitive to the complex and sophisticated. The earlier strands of biblical writing offered crude portrayals of God. As time went by, later writings evolved a more ethical and transcendent doctrine of God. Jesus stands as something of a pinnacle to biblical thought, with a much higher view of ethics than what had gone before. This evolutionary framework takes a dim view of the most ancient traditions of biblical history.

The second assumption of liberal Christianity is an anti-supernatural bias. Liberal theologians accepted the Enlightenment attitude to miracles: they did not happen. A miracle was not a historical event. It might reflect the confusion of a simple people who did not have access to scientific methods. Or it might be a fanciful story conveying spiritual truths. But whatever else a miracle is, it should not be defended as a historical event. This bias stripped Christianity of its supernatural claims. There was no parting of the sea at the time of Moses, no virgin birth, no multiplying of the loaves and fishes, and no physical resurrection. There might have been a historical event behind these miracle stories, but the two must be disentangled. Perhaps the early Hebrews did find a marshy crossing point somewhere on the Sea of Reeds which helped them escape Pharaoh's chariots. Perhaps the teaching of Jesus so inspired the crowds with generosity that they willingly shared the little they had each brought with them, and consequently found there was more than enough to go around. Perhaps the early followers of Jesus were so enamoured of their deceased leader that they projected a view of divinity upon him, expressed in stories of a miraculous birth and a bodily resurrection.

As an apologetic for Christianity, liberalism was fatally flawed. It achieved credibility at the price of integrity. The gospel the liberal theologians had made credible was not the gospel of historic Christianity. This raised a basic problem with the Enlightenment Age. The modern world had formed a materialistic worldview which was inherently hostile to the Christian faith. But conforming the Christian message to the spirit of the age was to destroy the message itself.

At best, God was an unnecessary embarrassment in the modernist worldview. At worst, he was a non-existent stumbling block. The rapid success of evolutionary theory as an explanation for our origins made reference to God rather superfluous. Darwin himself felt under pressure to include reference to a Creator at the close of *On the Origin of Species*, which appears in later editions.

Common-sense Christianity

There was an alternative approach to apologetics during this period that continued to maintain the historical foundations of Christianity. The roots of this alternative approach are to be found in the work of an apologist rarely referred to directly today, but worth remembering. Thomas Reid (1710–96) was a Scottish contemporary of David Hume. You may recall that it was Hume's sceptical approach to knowledge that had given Immanuel Kant the encouragement to develop his rationalist theory. All these Enlightenment ideas were based on the assumption that we could not be sure about metaphysical beliefs. Was there a God? Could there be miracles? Was there really such a thing as an external world, cause and effect or time itself? Kant was deeply troubled by Hume and this sceptical frame of mind. Thomas Reid was a Calvinist Christian who offered a quite different response to Hume. Reid pointed out that we believe many things as a matter of common sense. We all know that there is cause and effect, for example. Therefore, we should trust our common sense unless we have good reason not to do so. This was the opposite of the approach of the sceptics. Rather than doubting common sense until we have proof, which is silly and not something we do in ordinary life, we should trust common sense unless it is shown to be faulty. This approach to knowledge came to be called Common Sense Realism. For Reid, this was based on clear biblical principles. We are made in the image of God to live in a God-created universe.

Many of the positive developments in scientific discovery and research owe more to Common Sense Realism than to the scepticism of Kant and the European Enlightenment. Reid saw good reason to trust our senses, and it is on this basis that a great deal of experiment and discovery would be made. Many great Western scientists would owe much to the Reformation heritage.[8] Christianity provided good reasons to trust our common sense. We have been created by a faithful God who would not set out deliberately to deceive us. The material world around us is real, and we can generally trust our observations unless strong evidence suggests otherwise.

Modernism in decline

The term 'modern age' could be applied to any period which we consider to be the present. However, in intellectual terms it is generally used to describe a period that began with the philosophy of Descartes and its turn from the authority of church or state to personal authority. With its scientific discoveries, exploration and industrial revolution, the modern age bore fruit that benefited many. So has the modern age come to an end or is it still the age we live in? This is too complex a question to consider here, but we can see that the spirit of the modern age has been battered.

Optimism disappointed

Modernism held a high view of scientific discovery, and Enlightenment Western culture had an optimistic view of where the future would take us. At least during the early part of the twentieth century, there was a real sense in which humanity could do better without the entanglements of God and religion. However, that optimism was seriously undermined by the period after 1914 when the world was plunged into a period of two world wars in which the great achievements of scientists would include mustard gas, bomber planes, nuclear weaponry and the industrialized slaughter of six million Jews. It is interesting to note the reputation of the scientist in the white lab coat changing during this period. In the early years of the twentieth century, the white lab coat represented the scientific hero opening up a better world for the future. By the close of the Second World War, the white lab coat was the uniform of the evil genius, the nemesis of superheroes and a threat to human survival. Nuclear bombs, vivisection, ecological disasters and eugenics were all a part of scientific progress. No wonder blood pressures are thought to rise at the mere sight of someone in a white lab coat (dubbed 'white coat syndrome').

William Golding captures the fragility of the modern world in his novel *The Lord of the Flies*. Describing the survival of a group of children on a remote Pacific island, the story charts a downward spiral. The children quickly lose the veneer of ordered, civilized behaviour to become animal-like in their mistreatment of one another. Civilization has a thin veneer, and the beast soon emerges. Golding explained:

> Before the Second World War I believed in the perfectibility of social man; that a correct structure of society would produce goodwill . . . but after the war I did not because I was unable to. I had discovered what one man could do to another.[9]

Golding's observations were shared by many. The optimism of the modern age was shifting to a darker, bleaker view of the human spirit and the direction of civilization. Science fiction films and novels follow this trajectory. An earlier age had been optimistic about the achievements and possibilities of technology. A later age came to recognize its deeper flaws and weaknesses. With it came pessimism over the possibilities of science.

The death of God

Friedrich Nietzsche (1844–1900) is one of the most fascinating
critics of the Enlightenment Age. In many ways Nietzsche
occupies the difficult borderland between genius and insanity,
so his thought is not always presented in a logical, consistent
manner. His philosophical works include collections of what
we would today call 'soundbites'. These aphorisms can be
ambiguous and hard to smooth into a clear and comprehen-
sible worldview. But they do make him easy to read, and in
order to understand Western culture it is worth spending
some time with him.

As a young man, Nietzsche studied theology, but he lost his
faith in God primarily because of his study of the historical
background to Christianity. Turning to philosophy, Nietzsche
became scathing in his criticism of the Christian faith and what
he saw as the weak, 'spidery' God of Christ. But Nietzsche was
also severely critical of Kant.

Nietzsche's central criticism is quite profound. He recognized that an important foundation of Christianity had not
been demolished by the Enlightenment. While Kant and his
followers had dismissed the orthodox view of God, the supernatural and miracles, they had failed to grasp how far-reaching
the implications were for ethics. Consider the famous claim
that 'God is dead'. When Nietzsche penned these words, he
was not celebrating the triumphant conclusion to an
argument; he was describing the spiritual condition of the
modern age. God, indeed the gods, had died as a real part of
people's lives. Was this a good thing?

Have you not heard of the madman who lit a lantern in the
bright morning hours, ran to the market place, and cried
incessantly: 'I seek God! I seek God!' – As many of those who

did not believe in God were standing around just then, he provoked much laughter . . . 'Whither is God?' he cried; 'I will tell you.' *We have killed him* – you and I. All of us are his murderers. But how did we do this? How could we drink up the sea? . . . Are we not straying through an infinite nothing? Do we not feel the breath of empty space? Has it not become colder? Is not night continually closing in on us? Do we not need to light lanterns in the morning? Do we hear nothing as yet of the noise of the gravediggers who are burying God? Do we smell nothing as yet of the divine decomposition? Gods, too, decompose. God is dead. God remains dead. And we have killed him.[10]

Nietzsche was the madman with his lantern who declared his time had not yet come. This was no celebration or victory speech. In fact, Nietzsche describes it as a requiem for the dead. God was dead in the minds and hearts of the population. While still claiming faith in God, their lives betrayed a practical atheism. The implications of this murder were profound, and Nietzsche could see where they would lead. Christianity taught the absolutes of good and evil. Without faith in the God of Christianity, how did one have any basis for such moral absolutes? Nietzsche thought Kant had started well with his call to be free of external authorities, but he then found some other basis for God and morality, 'like a fox who loses his way and goes astray back into his cage'.[11] If there is no God, then there is no basis for absolute morality. Morality, like taste in art or food, becomes a subjective choice. After God's funeral, there would no longer be grounds to talk of absolute right and wrong, good and bad, beautiful and ugly. Society must be led beyond good and evil.

Nietzsche himself was a complex person who died relatively young, having suffered a mental breakdown. His legacy of contradictory claims and ambiguous statements has led to a wide spectrum of plaudits, from Adolf Hitler the founder of Nazism to Theodore Herzl a founder of the modern state of Israel. Nietzsche was a kind of visionary. He could foresee that in the twilight of religion we would not enter a world of endless optimism and progress. Instead, the heavy hand of religion would be replaced by the competing claims of rival ideologies. In his 1888 work, *The Anti-Christ*, Nietzsche presents his most virulent attack on Christianity. He denounces the religion for preserving weakness and pity. In his very last writings, he defines the uniqueness of his work as the unmasking of Christianity. At its heart is his repudiation of what he calls 'the Christian conception of God': 'God as God of the sick, God as spider, God as spirit . . . is one of the most corrupt conceptions of God arrived at on earth; perhaps it even represents the low-water mark in the descending development of the God type.'[12] Nietzsche hated and rejected the God of Christianity, but he also realized where this rejection would lead.

One day in 1889, towards the end of his life, Nietzsche saw a man cruelly mistreating a horse in the streets of Turin. Moved by pity, he ran to the horse and threw his arms around it in protection. Policemen found him collapsed in the street, and he never properly recovered. One might have thought this was an act of heroism, and in our contemporary culture with our sensitivity to animal welfare consider this an admirable act. Not Nietzsche. He considered it a failure of himself to live up to his principles. He had betrayed his philosophical convictions by acting in such a weak, compassionate manner. This raises the question: can we really live out our philosophy? Ahead of his time, Nietzsche heralded the demise of the modern age and the darker possibilities ahead.

Postmodernism

Postmodernism simply means whatever comes after (post) the modern age. The term developed among architects, but was quickly adopted to describe philosophy. Postmodernism is not simply an intellectual development – it reflects changes in culture, art, morality and education. It represents a shift in worldview. Douglas Rushkoff, a social commentator who celebrates this shift, puts it in these terms:

> Our children, ironically, have already made their move. They are leading us in our own evolution past linear thinking, duality, mechanism, hierarchy, metaphor, and God himself toward a dynamic, holistic, animistic, weightless, and recapitulated culture. Chaos is their natural environment.[13]

Postmodern philosophers have had most influence in the humanities: literature, media and theology have all nurtured outspoken postmodern thinkers. Postmodernists are sceptical of the great claims made by the Enlightenment. Don't all worldviews and truth claims involve a complex web of interpretation, vested interests and rhetoric? Following Nietzsche, postmodernists have taken the Enlightenment to its ultimate dead end. As Don Carson comments, 'The modernity which has arrogantly insisted that human reason is the final arbiter of truth has spawned a stepchild that has risen to slay it.'[14] If Descartes and Kant were correct to start with self-knowledge as the basis for all true knowledge, then ultimately there is nothing beyond the self to know. Modernism and postmodernism are two chapters in one story. As Lesslie Newbigin notes, 'The modern age began with the daring program of Descartes . . . Certainty was possible, and we ought to be content with nothing less. It is deeply ironic that this method has led us directly into the profound skepticism of the post-modern world.'[15] Even objectivity and rationality are no more than projections of our own inner thoughts. This is why Christians should be very wary of making the mistake apologists have made in the past of adopting a new cultural trend as their own.

Given the hostility of modernism to biblical faith, it might be tempting to join forces with postmodern responses. Some Christians have been urging just this. Philip Kenneson rejects traditional evangelical apologetics: 'Our efforts to argue people into the kingdom by insisting that what we are saying is objectively true reduce the Christian faith to a form of Gnosticism, and ironically, a modernist form of Gnosticism at that.'[16] Objective truth is dismissed as a modernist concept, and the apologetic task is for the church to be a 'living mystery'.[17] This may be a tempting strategy for Christians. We like to distance ourselves from arrogant, bold claims to absolute truth. Doesn't Christianity speak of realms beyond our understanding and ideas that may not be simple black and white? With questions like this, many Christians are drawn to adopt a postmodern stance. However, careful consideration of where these ideas have come from and what they really entail should trip the alarm bells.

The Gulf War did not take place. Apparently.

Jean Baudrillard (1929–2007) is a good representative of post-modern thought.[18] One of the key issues for him was the relationship between language and meaning. What Baudrillard, among many others, emphasized was that there is no intrinsic meaning in the words we use. Words have meaning only in relation to other words that we choose to use as a community. After his earlier years as a Marxist, Baudrillard dispensed with the ideas of modernism. His highly influential work, *Simulacra and Simulation*,[19] was first published in France in 1981 and marked a development in his understanding of post-modernism. Baudrillard argued that there is no such thing as reality (what could that be other than another word sign?). All we have is the simulated reality of signs in which we have no choice but to live. We never see things the way they are, but only the way they appear to us in our simulated reality. Baudrillard's work was directly influential on the Wachowski brothers in their production of *The Matrix* trilogy of films. Neo, the hero of the films, is shown in the opening scene storing a computer disk into a hollowed-out copy of *Simulacra and Simulation* which he keeps on his bookshelf. The films play on the idea that the general population live in a technologically generated virtual reality from which Neo will attempt a liberation.

Another key text from Baudrillard is actually a collection of three essays published in 1991 as *The Gulf War Did Not Take Place*. In the run-up to the first Gulf War in Iraq, he published 'The Gulf War Will Not Take Place' (4 January 1991). As the international armies began the assault on Iraq, he pursued his theme with 'The Gulf War: Is It Really Taking Place?' (6 February 1991). As Iraq surrendered and the war came to a close, he wrote 'The Gulf War Did Not Take Place' (29 March 1991). All three were then published together as a provocative book, setting out his theory. What did Baudrillard really mean? Our answer to that depends on how radical we understand postmodernism to be. Did Baudrillard deny that people, military and civilian, died in clashes in Iraq during 1991? The radical answer would be that we simply cannot say – we can only use these self-referential signifiers called words and never identify reality directly. However, this may not be entirely fair to Baudrillard.

Baudrillard never denied that people actually died in the fighting during 1991. What he argued is that our understanding of what was happening was a fiction created by the clever use of words in our technological age. Words such as 'war', 'armies' and 'surrender' helped to create an image of what was happening. But it was purely a creation of the media and the industrial and political systems for their own ends. The blanket media coverage offering the first twenty-four-hour continual broadcasting of an unfolding conflict gave the impression that we knew more about what was going on than in any previous conflict. Baudrillard thought differently. The barrage of information was itself overwhelming and needed to be placed in a framework for it to mean anything. The framework is provided for us by the media for its own reasons. Therefore, the meaning of the conflict is an interpretation foisted on us by those with political or economic advantages. Who can question these interpretations, given the mass of data that overwhelms us from cable news and the internet? 'We live in a world where there is more and more information, and less and less meaning.'[20]

So we are swamped by information, but lack a real sense of meaning. Did the Gulf War happen? Baudrillard says no. But he affirms that there was a slaughter in the Middle East during the early months of 1991. How that slaughter is interpreted depends on the agenda of those in power. As Marcus Honeysett notes in his engagement with postmodern authors, Baudrillard 'was writing ironically, to get people to react to the media presentation of the war'.[21] For Baudrillard, how something is said is just as important as what is actually said.

Postmodernism is often associated with relativism. Relativism accepts that the truthfulness of beliefs or ideas is relative to who we are and to our individual outlook on life.

Relativism in ethics means that there is no absolute right or wrong. Ethical decisions depend on our personal preferences and circumstances. Epistemological relativism means that our view of reality or truth itself depends on our personal outlook. Baudrillard is one of many thinkers to question what words such as 'reality' or 'truth' really mean. Are they simply ways of trying to state that our view is correct, to the detriment of any alternative? Is there such a thing as objective truth, or is truth simply a word to highlight our own personal preference? These questions are significant. They raise the possibility that we are using language in a manipulative way to pretend to be objective when we are really just pushing an agenda. This postmodern questioning has been very helpful in unmasking the prejudice of the Enlightenment Age. However, the post-modernist strategy fails because it ends up sawing off the very branch it is sitting on. One thing that is often pointed out is that the postmodernist is making claims about reality and pronouncing upon the views of others. Therefore, she is holding to an objective point of view when she makes claims about the bias of contemporary news reporting. In other words, relativism cannot go all the way; there must be some secure viewpoint. To be an absolute relativist would be to give up even the claim that relativism is true.

Relativism is easily faulted. No postmodernist is consistent. Again, Baudrillard provides a useful example. In his response to the Wachowski brothers' use of his work in *The Matrix* trilogy, he is dismissive:

Certainly there have been misinterpretations, which is why I have been hesitant until now to speak about *The Matrix* . . . Basically, a similar misunderstanding occurred in the 1980s when New York-based Simulationist artists contacted me. They took the hypothesis of the virtual for an irrefutable fact and transformed it into a visible phantasm. But it is precisely that we can no longer employ categories of the real in order to discuss the characteristics of the virtual.[22]

Why does he feel this way? Essentially, Baudrillard finds fault with the producers' interpretation of his work. *The Matrix* films use the idea of the simulation as a temporary trap for Neo and the general population, but then they allow our hero and his friends to escape the simulation and fight their counter-insurgency from the real world. The film fails to engage with any irony in the fact that as a film it is very much of a piece with the very things Baudrillard was so critical of. The idea that the virtual can be something we escape from and view from a distance, particularly in the form of a lavish Hollywood movie bloated on special effects, is far from the stance of *Simulation and Simulacra*. At least this is Baudrillard's problem with the movies. But herein lies the problem. If all reality is interpretation, then how can Baudrillard claim the Wachowski brothers got it wrong? Why should we prefer Baudrillard's interpretation of his work to that of the film directors? What gives him the right to dictate what is a good or bad, right or wrong, interpretation of his philosophy? Certainly, authorial intentions are not relevant here. This is a constant problem with postmodern thought. If all interpretations have validity, then why should a postmodernist complain that he or she feels misunderstood?

So is contemporary Western culture dominated by modernism or postmodernism? The fact is we live in a culture where there are many significant worldviews that jostle for attention. Increasingly, the worldview of Islam and Eastern religions has entered the fray. Nonetheless, the major influences on our media producers, writers, artists and thinkers remain the legacy of the past two hundred years. Some remain firmly committed to modernism, sceptical of anything supernatural, optimistic about the possibilities of scientific progress and convinced that the materialistic worldview can explain all of reality. Others are committed to postmodernism, sceptical of any absolute claims, pessimistic about scientific progress and convinced that no single worldview can explain all of reality. A postmodern author such as Jean Baudrillard is hard to take too seriously. Such authors challenge us to mistrust everything, but inspire little trust in their own claims. The very first quotation in *Simulation and Simulacra* claims to be from the book of Ecclesiastes, but is nowhere to be found there! Either Baudrillard has produced a very loose translation of his own or he just made it up. The latter is more likely, and so his own authority is diminished. But perhaps that's exactly the point a postmodern author like Baudrillard would want to make! As it appeared in the strapline to the hit science fiction series *The X-Files*: 'Trust no one. Question everything.' Nonetheless, the postmodern challenge is nothing more than a call to question. Christians can freely admit that we do not have the whole truth and must question received ideas. Isn't that what the Reformers did? Don't most evangelicals on campus and in workplaces around the world have to be willing to doubt the majority opinion and go against the flow? But to admit we do not have the whole truth does not entail conceding that we have no truth at all. Truth claims don't have to be exhaustively true in order to be true.

Post-postmodernism

So Christians should be neither modernists nor post-modernists. We live within the cultures in which we share our faith, but we can also distance ourselves from the ideas, values and prejudices that they promote. Against modernism, the

Christian wants to emphasize that there is supernatural revelation which provides a basis for true knowledge. Against postmodernism, the Christian will have confidence that, even though our insights will have been shaped by our culture, revelation provides us with the true perspective on the universe. This perspective is true not because of some abstract objective standard, but because the God who has spoken has made the universe that way.

The twentieth century witnessed the apparently terminal decline of the church in Western Europe. This is often viewed as a relatively recent thing, perhaps stemming from the post-war baby boomers of the sixties' sexual revolution. It is claimed that the church declined because it lost touch with a generation, was poorly managed or became old-fashioned. However, this is a superficial view. The statistics demonstrate that church decline in all the main Protestant denominations was underway by the middle of the nineteenth century. Surveys from 1851 demonstrate that people were turning away from the churches long before.[23] Sociologists explain this in various ways, but perhaps we need to highlight that the intellectual climate had changed. Just as the secular scientists were discovering more and more, the theologians and priests were believing less and less. It may not be a coincidence that the publication of the great work of the Enlightenment Age, *On the Origin of Species,* appeared about the time that church-going in the UK peaked. Rather than presenting a robust defence of the Christian faith and winning hearts and minds to the trustworthiness of the Bible, it does seem as if many in the church had married the spirit of the age. In doing so, they had sided with Nietzsche in arranging the most significant funeral in history. Some of the finest Christian intellectuals tried to develop a theology that was compatible with Enlightenment thought.

This project continues today in the work of those who propose a theology compatible with postmodernism. Among Christians there are many who endorse postmodernism and reject apologetics as belonging to the Enlightenment Age. Some, like Brian McLaren and Rob Bell, have done a service in reminding the church of our wider calling in engaging with the creative arts. But this can be achieved by returning to our roots. Apologists down the centuries have also done these things. It would be a travesty to imply that Lewis or Schaeffer had failed to engage with the creative arts. Postmodern Christianity has given up on defending absolute truth or winning debates. In doing so, it has robbed biblical faith of its heart and offered the world a decomposing corpse. In response to this decline, we can return to the positive and powerful tools at the disposal of Christians in sharing their faith in the contemporary world.

7. Digging up the Bible

History is philosophy teaching by examples.
Thucydides

It is a great irony that during the Enlightenment period there were developments in the sciences that helped confirm the trustworthiness of the Bible and the Christian faith at just the same time as many theologians and priests came to doubt it. Before we turn to the natural sciences, we will pause and consider the contribution of archaeology.

A load of rubbish

Archaeology is the study of the material remains of human history. From bones and flint tools to cities and roads, anything that is physical evidence of human existence is suitable subject matter. Generally, archaeology is rubbish. It is the study of the debris and litter left behind by a long-gone people.

Archaeology probably began as an attempt to find facts that confirmed the biblical record. Perhaps the first person who could lay claim to being a biblical archaeologist was the

Roman Emperor Constantine's mother. After Constantine (AD 274–337) legalized Christianity, his mother embarked on a quest for historical artefacts. Among her supposed finds was the cross of Jesus. However, her passions did not give rise to the reasonable study of archaeology so much as the super-stitious veneration of relics. There was a time when no church in the Western world was complete without a fragment of the holy cross or a bone of a deceased saint. It has been suggested that if all those fragments of the true cross were reassembled, they would create a cross large enough to execute a Roman legion.

The real beginnings of archaeology are found during the Enlightenment, when the great empires, especially those of Britain and France, brought relative stability across the world and allowed for careful scientific pursuit. During this time, Napoleon's army discovered the Rosetta Stone in Egypt (1799). French and British antiquarians (who would later be known as archaeologists) excavated Nineveh and Babylon during the 1840s, unearthing the remains of ancient palaces. Discoveries like these inspired curiosity about what might remain of other sites of biblical interest. Edward Robinson (1794–1863) was an American scholar who used the Bible as a guide in his explor-ation of what was then called Palestine. Many other scholars followed, such as Charles Warren, a British military captain, and Leonard Woolley (1880–1960), all sharing some conviction about the historical reliability of the biblical text. In the light of the Bible, they explored places such as Ur, Jericho and Jerusalem, bringing various treasures to light.[1]

However, there were flaws in the work of these enthusiastic pioneers, but through a process of trial and error methods did improve. The work of the French archaeologist Flinders Petrie (1853–1942) and the American William Foxwell Albright (1891–1971) laid the basis for archaeological methods still practised to this day. Their careful attention to the levels of remains (strata) that were excavated and the various pottery types found in different levels is now a cornerstone for archaeological investigation. These methods are now supplemented by a range of technological tools at the disposal of archaeologists, including aerial photography, magnetometers and carbon dating.

Proving the Bible

While early biblical archaeologists used the text as a guidebook (particularly books like Joshua and Acts with their wealth of geographical and historical comments), some contemporary archaeologists deeply distrust any claim based on the Bible.

Today there are two broad groups of biblical archaeologists with opposing convictions on these matters. They are sometimes called the 'maximalists' and the 'minimalists'. The maximalists are those who believe that the biblical record of Israel's history, at least from the time of the exodus, is generally reliable and confirmed by historical discoveries. The minimalists are those who credit little historical substance to the biblical narrative prior to the seventh century BC. Many doubt the existence of Moses, Joshua or King David. The stories of the exodus, conquest and united monarchy are described as legends or myths to explain the origins of a people group. Perhaps surprisingly, there are even Israeli archaeologists who maintain the minimalist position and distrust the historical reliability of the biblical record. To be more accurate, most archaeologists do not fit either position. They recognize the ambiguity of the archaeological evidence and affirm that the Bible contains many useful insights into the past. Most of those categorized as minimalists are not archaeologists at all, but sociologists interpreting this evidence

at a distance – often much to the displeasure of the archaeologists in the field!

Apologists will want to affirm a more positive case for the
Bible, and there are good grounds to do so. In fact, archaeology provides more help in substantiating the reliability of
the Bible today than it has ever done. However, it is at this
point that we need to be cautious about the limits of archaeology and what we are trying to prove.

Many Christians are led into fringe archaeology in their
desire to prove the Bible. A good example is the claim
regarding the supposed discovery of the remains of Noah's
ark near Mount Ararat. This claim has a long history and is
not entirely an urban legend.

The modern story finds roots in the discovery made by a
Turkish army captain of an enormous boat-like rock formation
in the mountain region of Ararat, eastern Turkey. It was while
examining aerial photographs that this man had noticed the
unusual shape of the rock, and the subsequent publicity led to
a scientific investigation. The first survey revealed that the size
of the formation matched the dimensions of the Genesis
account, though not the shape (the ark described in Genesis is
more the shape of a canal barge than a traditional boat).
Further investigations followed, and most notably for evangelicals a young American, Ron Wyatt, visited the site and
reported back not only evidence for Noah's ark, but also rocks
that might have been its massive anchors, and the remains of
the house, altar and farm that Noah and his family had built.

Wyatt was probably better at publicity than many of the
other expedition leaders who had travelled to the Ararat
region and claimed to have found traces of the ark. However, the fact is that the stories sound a lot more convincing
than the hard evidence. The reality is that no clear photograph
or scientific test has demonstrated the existence of a large boat

in the region. And the photograph that is most commonly shown is misleading. Closer inspection demonstrates it to be a geological formation. The wealth of hard evidence that expeditions claimed to have found has been difficult for third parties to analyse – in fact much of it has gone missing, including artefacts, scientific reports, photographs and film. But Ron Wyatt was a busy man. Working only in his vacations, he also claimed to have found the stone tablets of the Ten Commandments, remains of Christ's blood with DNA results to prove he was born of a virgin, the site of the Red Sea crossing, including the remains of the Egyptian chariots, and the ark of the covenant, found by digging under the site of the temple. All the items on the list share the feature of offering great stories but little hard evidence. Their place in apologetics is counterproductive.

The remains of Noah's ark may still lie waiting to be dis-covered, buried beneath a glacier on Mount Ararat, but the story above serves as a warning. Wishful thinking must not cloud our judgment. Archaeology offers only tentative evidences, and there are important reasons why we would not expect direct evidence of many biblical events. For one thing, very little direct evidence of any events in ancient history has been found. Artefacts tend to decay, or get stolen, broken, melted down, recycled and forgotten. Sites tend to be built upon, reused and renamed as the centuries pass. Even events and historical figures from only a few hundred years ago are hard to prove without references in literature.

The right use of archaeology in apologetics will be cautious. Artefacts are useful for the light they cast on what we know from biblical history. We will expect them to agree with the general picture presented by the Bible. However, we will admit the limitations of what such finds can prove. Our priority is to demonstrate that faith in the Bible as reliable history is compatible with everything we know from archaeology rather than proven by what we know from archaeology. That sounds a little less alluring, but it is far wiser! Apologists should be cautious of giving the impression that faith can be based upon the shifting interpretations of archaeologists, as otherwise Christians may be left at the mercy of changing assessments of the artefacts.

Evidentialist apologists tend to make the most obvious use of archaeological discoveries in presenting the reliability of the Bible, but presuppositional apologists are very useful here too. They remind us that the evidence unearthed from the ground needs interpretation, and such interpretation is never purely objective.

The cultural context of Genesis

One of the most obvious apologetic challenges to the biblical text arises from the first eleven chapters of Genesis and concerns the relationship of the Bible to science. Is the creation account credible? Direct evidence for the events described in the early chapters of Genesis is not available. The events are too distant in time. And two points are worth taking into account in any defence of the historicity of the early chapters of Genesis.

First, the historical narrative is selective. Genesis is not a record of everything we might want to know about early human history. It does not tell us about the migration of the aborigines of Australia, the discovery of fire or the invention of the wheel. Events that would be important to the secular historian might be ignored in Genesis. What the book records are events that are key in the history of God's dealings with people, from the garden in Eden, through the flood, to the tower of Babel.

Secondly, the account is not undermined or untenable on the basis of anything we know from ancient history. Genesis describes people living to great ages. This is a feature shared with other ancient histories. Perhaps such ages are a literary style of writing or they may reflect a different way of calculating a person's age. Or perhaps Genesis shares with other documents a memory of time when people had a more durable constitution and could live to greater ages. In this latter case, it is interesting to contrast the Genesis account with parallels from outside the Bible. The ages recorded in Genesis are in the hundreds rather than the thousands recorded elsewhere. The account in Genesis is therefore far more sober than parallel accounts from the ancient world. It is far more plausible than the accounts that emerge among her neighbours.

Not only Genesis but other cultures of Mesopotamia recorded a great flood in ancient times. The Sumerians kept careful records of their kings and divided them between those who lived before the flood and those who lived after it. One of the earliest examples of literature is the Babylonian Epic of Gilgamesh, which includes an extensive account of a great flood sent by the gods as a punishment, a Mesopotamian 'Noah' called Utnapishtim, and an ark in which the animals were preserved. Similar stories are scattered throughout the ancient world. The evidential value of this material must be handled with care. It could be argued that there were many ancient floods – especially at the end of the Ice Age – and that one or two similar stories simply did the rounds and fitted with the collective memories of ancient cultures. What these stories do demonstrate, however, is that the Genesis record fits with what we know from outside of the Genesis account. As part of our presentation of the case for taking this text seriously, that is enough to warrant a hearing.

As the book of Genesis unfolds, we encounter a bewildering array of obscure place names, people and cultural practices.[2] Yet these all fit with what we know of that time in the ancient world. The period of the Patriarchs (Abraham, Isaac and Jacob) fits with what archaeologists call the Middle Bronze Age II (c. 2000–1550 BC). Cities like Laish, Dothan and Shechem were all thriving at this time. Names such as Abram and Asher were in use outside the Bible at this time. The name Phicol (Genesis 21:22) is not Hebrew but Hittite and belongs to that early era.

One of the very common objections to the reliability of the Old Testament is its supposed anachronisms: names or practices that belong to a later period that have been projected back into the past. Some anachronisms are acceptable – for example an editor might update a place name with its current usage rather than its ancient usage in order to aid understanding. This is little different from translating Scripture. However, a popular critical example is the presence of domesticated camels at the time of Abraham. The claim is that camels were not domesticated for another 800 years, and so the descriptions in Genesis are not reliable (i.e. Genesis 12:16; 31:17). However, this objection is itself out of date. There are examples of pottery camel figurines that would have carried loads from across the region which date to this period. A later example found in Arabia is even described by scholars as 'Midianite' ware (cf. Genesis 37:25).[3] While it is true that there is not an abundance of evidence, there is enough evidence to show that camels were beginning to be domesticated and were used to carrying loads from before the time of the Patriarchs. While not as common as donkeys and cattle, they were certainly at work in the countryside. Archaeological remains tend to cluster around urban environments where donkeys and cattle are found.

Camels were used to make the long-distance journey along trade routes far from the towns.

Moses and the exodus

Events surrounding the exodus were set at a time when more historical records were being kept, and these records are still available. The events not only concerned Israel's history, but impinged on the history of one of the great empires of the ancient world: Egypt. Given this context, it is reasonable to expect more direct evidence for the historical claims of the Bible.

The first problem we have is to establish when the exodus events took place. The Bible itself gives its own dating, which is generally reckoned to mean that the Israelites left Egypt during the fifteenth century BC. This is based on trusting the literal accuracy of the years recorded in the biblical account. A basis for dating the exodus is provided in 1 Kings 6:1. The event recorded in the fourth year of Solomon's reign can be established as having taken place in 967 BC (calculated by adding up the reigns of the kings who followed Solomon which are given in some detail through 1 and 2 Kings). Therefore, by simple arithmetic, the exodus took place in 1446 BC. This dating could be corroborated by adding together the reigns of the previous two kings: forty years for David, forty years for Saul, 360 years for the time of the judges and forty years of wandering in the wilderness. By this more circuitous route, we come to the same date for the exodus.

Other scholars question whether the dates and numbers provided in Scripture are to be taken so literally. Perhaps they are ideal numbers and symbolic patterns: especially significant is the period of forty years which represents a generation.

Many notable scholars prefer a later dating for the time of the exodus. A particularly important reason for this is the general consensus that Ramesses II was the pharaoh of the exodus, and he reigned from 1279 to 1213 BC. The Bible itself provides no name for the pharaoh, though it does give the name of one of the store cities built by the Hebrew slaves as 'Rameses' (Exodus 1:11; probably Pi-Ramesse), a hint of who the Pharaoh may have been. Ramesses I had a very brief reign and is not associated with any significant building projects. However, Ramesses II enjoyed an unusually long reign and was involved in major building work. Recent archaeological excavations at Qantir have revealed a major store city which may have been Pi-Ramesse. Archaeological evidence for the migration of new settlers into Canaan after this time also helps to bolster the claim.

However, there are circumstantial reasons for taking the earlier date for the exodus as more likely. The leadership of Egypt had just emerged from a period of foreign rule. The Hyksos rulers had come to an end and had been expelled from Egypt. The Hyksos were a foreign people of Semitic origins who entered Egypt during the Middle Bronze Age. Various attempts by the native Egyptians to overthrow their rule continued over two hundred years (1750–1550 BC). The period of Hyksos rule would coincide with the time of Joseph serving in the Egyptian court and the first Hebrew family settling in the land. If the rulers of that time were not pure-bred Egyptians, then it is quite plausible that nomads from Canaan would have had access to the corridors of power in Egypt. Being of Semitic origins, the Hyksos would have provided a favourable racial climate for Joseph and his family. However, the period of oppression would follow after the expulsion of the Hyksos when a new pharaoh emerged who didn't know Joseph (Exodus 1:8). The racial climate had changed. With

Semitic rulers destroyed or expelled, Joseph's ancestors would have become unwelcome aliens in the land.

In the wake of the exodus at its earliest date, there is a period of Egyptian history dubbed the 'Amarna heresy'. This refers to the short-lived attempt of Pharaoh Akhenaton (c. 1352–1336 BC) to impose a form of monotheism on to the Egyptian people. Their previous polytheism was abolished, and the capital city moved. In its ruins were found the cuneiform tablets now known as the Amarna Letters, including correspondence from rulers of Canaanite towns. They reflect the apparent weakness of Egyptian power during this time, as marauding invaders threatened the local kings and tribal chiefs. What was the impetus for Egypt to abandon its traditional polytheism, adopt a form of monotheism and lose the military capacity to support the outer reaches of its realm? Something like the exodus narrative could supply a plausible scenario.

Nothing here proves the date of the exodus – early or late – but it does demonstrate that there is nothing in the archaeological record that would make the exodus implausible. The circumstantial evidence provides a suitable context for what we read in the Bible.[4]

Our discussion of the exodus highlights a number of important points about ancient history relevant to apologetics:

1. Ancient history is generally recorded to celebrate success, not remember defeat. History is selective in many ways. A catastrophic defeat, such as the destruction of Pharaoh's chariots in pursuit of fleeing slaves, would not be one to remember! Nor are the names of enemy kings generally recorded (with some exceptions). The point of the historical record is to bring glory to the empire's own monarch, not provide

accurate records of who the rival kings and nations may have been.

2. History in the ancient world was close in form to propaganda. A striking example relevant to our case is found in the British Museum. A large hieroglyphic king list from the time of Ramesses II appears to be a list of pharaohs in their chronological order, providing the record of kings down to the time of Ramesses. However, from other records, we know that a number of kings are missing from the list, including the infamous Akhenaton, the heretic king. Those who drew up the list chose to exclude from the record what they did not want remembered. The Egyptian records are hardly likely to provide direct reference to the exodus.

These two points are relevant to our more general use of historical evidences in apologetics. We need to be aware of the way history is written. This does not mean that we cannot trust historical records, but it does mean that we have to recognize that the authors write with motives of their own and select material according to their personal purposes.

Furthermore, this reinforces the very important point that the absence of evidence does not constitute evidence of absence. In other words, just because we have not found direct evidence of an event or personality from the ancient world does not mean that it is not historical. Perhaps the evidence has not survived or has not yet been found.

Historical records of biblical events

So it is ironic that during the past two hundred years a great deal of scepticism has developed within biblical studies over the reliability of the Bible, while archaeological study has multiplied reasons for trusting its history. The theological traditions of Schleiermacher and Harnack tended to dismiss the ancient traditions of the Bible as mythological or super-stitious. But the developing science of archaeology leads in quite a different direction. A number of finds have overturned previously sceptical attitudes to the biblical record. It seems increasingly obvious that those who are dismissive of the biblical stories rely more on prejudice than on science.

The Hittites (literally 'Children of Heth') are mentioned a number of times in the Old Testament, including reference to their origins (Genesis 10:15), Abraham buying land from them (Genesis 23), and the geographical extent of their land (Joshua 1:4). Ahimelech and Uriah were well-known Hittites of the Old Testament. However, outside of the Bible, little evidence for the existence of the Hittites was known until the later nineteenth century. Enough literary evidence from Egypt and Assyria was coming to light to show their existence, but the descriptions found in the Bible were suspect. This scepticism is evident in the ninth edition of the *Encyclopaedia Britannica* (published from 1875) in an entry on the subject by Thomas Kelly Cheyne, who contrasted the Bible unfavourably with literature from Egypt and Assyria and generally dismissed the historical value of the biblical accounts.

In 1884, an inscription found at excavations in Turkey identified the location as the lost city of the Hittites (Hattusa). This discovery was quickly followed by further material evidence, cuneiform literature and connections to what was already known from Syria and Egypt. In 1906, a vast archive of documents was found at Hattusa which has clarified the history and customs of this forgotten people.

Today a great deal is known about the Hittites who had an extensive empire in what is now called Turkey and experienced significant conflicts with the Egyptians and the Assyrians. Their period of greatest influence was from 1750 to 1180 BC. They never occupied Canaan but their empire bordered this territory, and there is no reason to doubt that numerous Hittite families and individuals settled in Canaan from around the time of Abraham to the conquest under Joshua. It is true that a name like 'Uriah' does not seem Hittite in origin.[5] However, it is entirely to be expected that a Hittite living among the Hebrews would have adopted a name in keeping with his adoptive community, just as Daniel was given a Babylonian name in the exile.

What is most striking about the references to the Hittites in the early books of the Bible is that they appear in the correct period of early biblical history. Their empire came to an end by the eleventh century BC. This undermines the claim that the biblical accounts were written hundreds of years later.

A similar pattern of doubt and resolution can be found in the treatment of a biblical character called Belshazzar. He was the king of Babylon at the time of its fall, as recorded in the book of Daniel. The ancient Greek historians, Xenophon and Herodotus, provide comprehensive histories of the fall of Babylon, but do not supply the name of Belshazzar. During the rise of more critical treatments of the historicity of the Bible, this fuelled scepticism over the historical value of the book of Daniel. Perhaps the book was really the product of a zealous Jewish imagination telling a story three hundred years after the time in which the story was supposed to have been set? Perhaps Belshazzar was a fictional character or just a mistake in the record?

However, an archaeological discovery in 1854 brought Belshazzar to life and also helped in the interpretation of Daniel. It came in the form of a clay cylinder carrying a royal prayer declaring that Belshazzar was a co-regent with King

Nabonidus. More than a crown prince, the son of Nabonidus was entrusted with the rule of the kingdom during the king's ten-year absence. This casts useful light on the words of Belshazzar in Daniel 5:29. Having convincingly interpreted the appearance of supernatural writing, Daniel's wisdom is recognized, and he is proclaimed 'third highest ruler in the kingdom'. Why only third highest? Why not second in command? Belshazzar had no authority to grant Daniel a position higher than third, as he himself was only second in command. King Nabonidus, somewhere out of town, continued to claim the top spot.

Today no-one doubts the existence of Belshazzar in Babylon or Hittites in Canaan.[6] Those who doubted the reliability of the biblical text were allowing the absence of evidence to count as evidence of absence. Their doubts have since been dispelled, but the grounds of their doubts were always tenuous.

When did the people of Israel come to exist in some internationally recognized form? The claim of the minimalists is that only slowly did a tribal unity emerge among pastoral peoples in the Canaanite hill country. Sometime in the later Iron Age (after 700 BC) people created legends and myths of their origins as a unified people emerging out of slavery from Egypt. Again, a silence in the archaeological record could be interpreted as demonstrating the legendary status of ancient Israel. This sceptical view has been seriously undermined by a number of unexpected archaeological finds helping to date the emergence of Israel.

The first notable find is called the Israel or Merneptah Stela. A stela is a memorial inscription generally carved on stone which could function for many different purposes, including gravestones or commemorations. This particular stela was found in 1896 in Thebes, and it recorded the various victories of Pharaoh Merneptah (1213–1203 BC), noting many places that Merneptah conquered, and included a single, significant claim that 'Canaan is captive . . . Israel is wasted, bare of seed.' The name 'Israel' has a particular hieroglyphic form that refers to a people group rather than a geographical location, bolstering the claim that it is a reference to a people who may have settled throughout Canaan. Flinders Petrie, the archaeologist who discovered the Stela in Egypt, immediately grasped its significance, commenting that it would become his best-remembered find. It is the earliest reference to Israel and provides direct evidence that Israel existed as a significant people group already by the thirteenth century BC. It provides positive evidence for an early-date exodus and for the emergence of a distinct Israelite people, long before the emergence of a united monarchy.

The 4-foot-high Mesha Stele (sometimes known as the Moabite Stone) is today displayed in the Louvre, Paris. It was found in 1868 and details the victories of Mesha, a king of Moab, some time before 853 BC. Among the achievements is a reference to Omri and Ahab, kings of Israel. This is further positive proof of the early existence of Israel and their settlement of the land. Alongside ancient Assyrian inscriptions which mention Omri, Jehu and Ahab, there is a wealth of direct extra-biblical witness to the existence of kings described in the biblical record.

There is even indirect extra-biblical evidence for the existence of King David. The Tel Dan Stela was a chance discovery at the archaeological excavation of Old Testament Dan (formerly the city of Laish). Two fragments of a single stela bore an inscription in Old Aramaic, probably by Hazael, king of Damascus, claiming credit for the death of two Hebrew leaders. Significantly, he refers to both the king of Israel, Joram, and to the king of the House of David, Ahaziah. That these two kings both perished at around the same time during the reign of Hazael of Damascus is the claim of Scripture (2 Kings 9:1–29), and here it finds extra-biblical confirmation. The broken stela was discovered among the stones forming a wall in ancient Dan – evidence that recycling was an ancient preoccupation. But the archaeologists who chanced upon it recognized its enormous importance in the reference it bore to the 'House of David'. This was the earliest material reference to King David ever found. Recording events little more than a century after the lifetime of David, it established his historicity as the ancestor of a southern monarchy. King David could no longer be dismissed as if he were a legendary King Arthur of Canaan.

Further confirmation of the personalities and context of Old Testament history was brought to light by a British archaeological expedition in Mesopotamia, led by a twenty-eight-year-old rising archaeologist, Austin Henry Layard. Layard excavated the mound of Nimrud on the banks of the Tigris River in 1846. Then under the control of the Ottoman Turks, what would one day become the modern state of Iraq was a difficult and dangerous place in which to pursue archaeology. However, the excavations brought to light an enormous quantity of material remains from Assyrian civilization. The discovery of a number of palaces yielded important statues and wall reliefs, many of which would find their way back to London and the British Museum. Among the discoveries was an obelisk dating to the reign of the Assyrian King Shalmaneser III (859–824 BC). The beautifully detailed pictures and cuneiform inscriptions on this obelisk would provide important insights into the ancient world. The carvings depict various leaders bringing tribute to King Shalmaneser. Prominent among them is King Jehu with the Israelites bringing 'silver, gold, a golden bowl, a golden vase, golden tumblers, golden buckets, tin, a staff for a king [and] hunting

spears' in c. 841 BC.[7] This is the earliest pictorial image yet
found of the Israelites. It dates to an early period of the
divided monarchy (cf. 2 Kings 10), and illustrates that already
by the mid-ninth century BC they were one of the important
regional nations.

Manuscripts matter

There are many ancient Hebrew inscriptions which provide
evidence for the people and places of the Old Testament.
From cuneiform tablets, ostraca and commemorative stele,
we can piece together the existence and significance of ancient
Israel. More strikingly still, there are inscriptions or documents
which themselves cite Old Testament texts and show how
little it has changed over time. This is an important contribution of material archaeology because it has only served
to undermine one of the most influential critical theories
about the text of the Old Testament. This theory is that the
Hebrew Bible is a very late assemblage of various sources,
only appearing in the form we know it long after the events
which it was supposed to have described. Many scholars
developed elaborate theories about the sources and how
they had been welded together by later editors. In particular,
the Pentateuch, or first five books of the Bible, was an
amalgamation of four different sources which only found one
another in the fifth century BC. They were attributed to Moses
a thousand years after he was supposed to have lived. This
kind of theory has many variations, but is often taken to imply
the unhistorical nature of the texts. However, it is important
to point out that the source theory is a literary theory, based
exclusively on assumptions about the text that we have before
us. There is no material evidence that the Bible was composed
in this fashion. In fact, the material evidence that does emerge

from the ancient world actually demonstrates the antiquity of the Old Testament.

Dead Sea documents

The Dead Sea forms in the lowest point on earth, where a great geological rift works its way down from Syria in the north to Africa. From the western shore of the Dead Sea, a desert terrain forms and climbs its way up to Jerusalem in the north-west. This is the wilderness region in which we know David and Jesus wandered. It is a dry and demanding terrain, with sparse vegetation, but communities did settle there, and two thousand years after their dispersal, one separatist group of Jewish men, called the Essenes, would even become world famous.

The Dead Sea community were diligent students of the Hebrew Bible and lived an ascetic life of contemplation in the desert region. They did not worship with the Jews at the Jerusalem temple, but formed their own reclusive religious society. A key feature of community life was the copying of Old Testament scrolls and producing texts of their own, including commentaries on Old Testament books. In AD 68, the Roman army under General Vespasian engaged in suppressing a revolt of the Jews in Palestine which would culminate in the destruction of the temple in Jerusalem. Probably during this time, the community at Qumran was destroyed, the ruined buildings then serving as a temporary base for the Romans as they laid siege to the fortress of Masada. Excavations at Masada revealed pieces of scrolls from the Qumran community, suggesting that many may have fled there, carrying with them some of their scrolls.

But the community hid many of their treasured scrolls in caves near to their monastery. This simple act would in time come to be of great benefit to us, because the climate of this wilderness area, while forbidding for wildlife, is perfect for the preservation of manuscripts. The chance discovery of the first scrolls nearly two thousand years later in 1947 had enormous implications for apologetics.

The Dead Sea Scrolls comprised over 800 scrolls found in eleven different caves. Among them every book of the Old Testament has been found, with the exception of Esther, along with many other texts. They are all now translated and published, and they cast light on the context of first-century Palestine. They also provide clear documentary evidence for the faithfulness of the copying of the Hebrew Scriptures. Prior to their discovery, the earliest complete Old Testament in Hebrew was the rather unromantically designated Leningrad B19a, or Masoretic Text, copied in AD 1009. It helps scholars to compare contemporary versions with early manuscripts to ensure they have been faithfully copied over the centuries. There were, of course, a number of fragments and sections from the years prior to the tenth century AD, but the discovery of the Dead Sea Scrolls allowed scholars to leap back a further thousand years in time to test the faithfulness of scribal copying.

A complete scroll of the book of Isaiah was found at Qumran and was probably copied c. 100 BC. It was already an old manuscript when the library was sealed away in the caves. Scholars could now compare the Masoretic Text with a complete text of Isaiah copied over a thousand years earlier. Despite its great length, there are only a few minor variations. For example, the Revised Standard Version translation made thirteen word changes to the book of Isaiah based on this manuscript discovery. However, later editions reduced this to three changes.[8] The faithful preservation of the text is beautifully confirmed by this chance discovery on the cliffs above the Dead Sea.

Discoveries continue to be made. Before the close of the twentieth century, a find less in quantity but equal in quality to the Dead Sea Scolls would emerge. Two small silver scrolls were found in a burial chamber just outside Jerusalem in 1979 by an archaeological team led by Gabriel Barkay. Unrolling the fragile scrolls was a slow, painstaking process, but yielded the oldest written Bible verses yet found. Dating to 600 BC or earlier, the scrolls, called the Ketef Hinnom amulets, were found to bear the Hebrew text of Numbers 6:22–26, which included the divine name 'Yahweh'. This was only the start. Further testing confirmed the early dating of the scrolls and revealed yet more Hebrew letters. These inscriptions at least parallel other biblical texts, but a further direct citation is found of Deuteronomy 7:9. These findings have only very recently come to light and have benefited from advances in computing and optical technology. They lend weight to the integrity and age of the texts of the Old Testament. These findings do not fit with the out-of-date theories of source criticism. We have material evidence to suggest that texts found in Numbers and Deuteronomy were already in circulation together and recognized as Scripture by 600 BC – much earlier than the liberal sceptics had thought.

The evidence for the textual reliability of the Bible is very strong. Finds have confirmed the trustworthiness of the text. Not a single find has emerged that provides any evidence for the classic source theory of German scholarship.

Summary

We can summarize this chapter in terms of four key themes for apologetics:

1. **The importance of history.** History is the context in which God has spoken and acted. The biblical worldview puts

a high value on the meaning, purpose and value of history. Therefore, historical claims and evidences will always matter to Christians and be important in their apologetics. This lends itself to the evidentialist approach to apologetics with its concern for historical evidences. However, all apologists share this concern to demonstrate the reliability of the Bible, and counter the biased prejudice against taking the Bible seriously for its historical content.

2. **Limitations of historical studies.** Biblical events took place long ago over an extended time-frame, and much of the relevant material evidence will have long since disappeared. In fact, literary records like the Old Testament are themselves an important way of accessing ancient history. This is not only true for ancient Israel but for all ancient cultures. The archaeological record is very patchy and relies on a great deal of interpretation. We must be aware that absence of evidence is not necessarily evidence of absence. The wilderness wandering of Israel, and even the crossing of the Sea of Reeds, are not likely to have left anything substantial in the archaeological record. Historical studies help to provide a context for what we read in the Bible and provide good reason to trust the general reliability of the texts.

3. **Confirmation of biblical events.** Sometimes an event in the Bible can be directly confirmed by secular sources. The siege of Jerusalem under the Assyrians would be a good example from the Old Testament (2 Kings 18 – 19). An Assyrian record of the same event helps to build a picture of the historicity of Scripture. If we find the Bible reliable where it can be tested, then we have good reason to trust it in those places where it cannot be tested. In many places where the Bible had been dismissed as inaccurate, later discoveries have reinstated its reliability. There is nothing irrational about assuming that this is quite possible in other areas of dispute.

4. **Specific finds.** A vast number of specific material discoveries have been made that are of great value in apologetics. Christians should remember a number of significant ones that are of interest to them and be able to share their importance with friends. This helps demonstrate our enthusiasm for the history and reliability of the Bible. However, we should share the secular historian's suspicion of unprovenanced finds and more sensational claims. The credibility of our witness can be undermined when supposed evidence turns out to be either misinterpreted or faked. There are plenty of widely accepted and extensively researched finds which demonstrate the credibility of the Bible. Christians ought to have some familiarity with examples such as the Merneptah Stela, the Black Obelisk of Shalmaneser III, the period of Akhenaton and the Dead Sea Scrolls. The study of these artefacts and our understanding of these periods have developed during the last century, and they substantiate our claim to the reliability of the Bible.

The Age of the Enlightenment has brought huge strides forward in historical and archaeological studies. Whatever the claims of radical philosophers or theologians, Christians have a growing body of positive evidence with which to become familiar in their apologetic for the faith.

8. Science friction

*Science, when understood properly, makes
man humble in his ignorance and smallness.*
Time Magazine, 1965

The conflict myth

In our survey of the development of the modern age, the
rise of contemporary science features very prominently.
This has been the age of science and discovery, something
which has brought Christians many challenges, though we
should never forget that Christians have themselves been at
the forefront of this age of discovery. One of the main lines of
defence for the Christian faith uses the evidence of science.
However, one of the main lines of attack on Christianity also
uses the evidence of science. So is science a friend or a foe? It
seems that it can be used either way, and this should alert us
to the likelihood that we are not just dealing with brute facts.

Before we explore this theme, it is worth making it very
clear that the image of science and religion in conflict is a
popular misunderstanding. Many leading scientists past and
present have been, and are today, believers, while others have

been sceptics. Disputes over any significant scientific theory have never been simply conflicts between believers and doubters. Historic scientists who have also been believers include Galileo, Copernicus and Asa Gray (a friend and defender of Darwin in America). None of these scientists just happened to be Christians because of the culture they were part of. They were all thoughtful, active Christians who also gave time to write on subjects of theological concern.

Contemporary history continues to witness the active engagement of Christians with science. Alister McGrath refers to a survey carried out in 1916 and repeated in 1996. The same question was asked of practising scientists: did they believe in a personal God to whom one could pray in expectation of an answer? When the same survey was carried out eighty years later, the results were almost unchanged. The number of those who did not believe had risen from 40% to 45%, while the number who did believe remained 40%.[1] Therefore it is reasonable to conclude that whether or not one has faith in God is not determined simply by scientific evidence. There is a far more important issue of worldview and the way scientists interpret the evidence.

Far from being in conflict, natural sciences and theology are distinct, though overlapping, areas of knowledge. A striking example of this is found in John Calvin's commentary on the first chapter of Genesis. At the time of writing, Nicholas Copernicus had offered a new view of the solar system. Instead of the medieval view, in which the earth was at the centre with the sun and planets revolving around us, Copernicus was led through observation to conclude that the sun was at the centre. Many church officials had problems with what was called the 'Copernican revolution'. Didn't the Bible describe the sun as rising and setting while earth remains fixed and immobile? Astronomy was developing an image of the solar system quite different from the one you might imagine if you had only the material in the first book of the Bible at your disposal. Commenting on the first chapter of Genesis, Calvin notes that 'it is not here philosophically discussed, how great the sun is in the heaven, and how great, or how little is the moon . . . For as it became a theologian, [Moses] had respect to *us* rather than to the *stars*.'[2] In other words, Genesis describes how things appear to us and why God made them that way, rather than giving the relative planetary sizes in terms of astronomy. Astronomy and other sciences are valid pursuits, but should be distinguished from theology.

Of course, there is an important issue here of how the book of Genesis is to be interpreted. Evangelical Christians of great scholarship are divided. The view a Christian takes of the opening chapters of Genesis will clearly determine how he or she answers some of these difficult questions. How old is the earth? Did human beings evolve from earlier hominids? Was there cancer and death prior to the fall? The creationist movement argues that these are fundamental questions. We must answer them in order to provide a coherent account of the gospel. However, I would urge caution here. Given that intelligent, sincere believers have different views and that many change their minds, it is unwise to create an unnecessary stumbling block by suggesting a non-Christian need endorse a particular interpretation of Genesis before becoming a Christian. However, the broader argument from design is a key component of Christian apologetics.

The argument from design

Christians have always appealed to the grandeur or complexity of creation as evidence of the existence of God. Even if this is not offered as a logical argument, we often assume many people share the nagging feeling that there is more to the world than meets the eye. Cicero (106–43 BC), the pagan Roman thinker, asked,

> When you look at a sun-dial or a water clock, you consider that it tells the time by art and not by chance; how then can it be consistent to suppose that the world, which includes both the works of art in question, the craftsmen who made them, and everything else besides, can be devoid of purpose and reason?[3]

Plato and Aristotle both offer some form of an argument from a first cause. The chain of cause and effect cannot disappear into the past without end; there must be some agency (a first cause) that began the process.

We have already seen how Thomas Aquinas sought to demonstrate the existence of God by inference from common-sense beliefs through his 'five ways' or proofs. The first of these uses our understanding of motion. All things we see are in motion, and this can be traced like a chain of things in motion to an Unmoved Mover. The second way follows a chain of causes backwards from the effects we see to the causes of those effects. It's a bit like watching a ball rolling; we immediately wonder what made the ball roll. We could follow that kind of series back through many steps, but we expect it to come to an end at some point with a first cause of the ball rolling. The third and fourth ways are more philosophical in their form, to do with God being a necessary and perfect being. The fifth way is an argument from the apparent purpose in the natural order. This is what is meant by a teleological argument. *Telos* is a Greek word meaning 'end' or 'purpose'. Wherever we see purpose, there is evidence of a directing hand, and this is thought to be the hand of God. Evidence of design is evidence for a designer.

David Hume, the eighteenth-century sceptic, launched an important counter-argument to this line of thinking. He used the existence of evil, or design flaws, as arguments against the existence of the God of the Bible. Perhaps there was a designer, or designers, but they could be irrational forces or evil demigods in a battle with one another. At most, the argument from design indicates the existence of some cosmic law which may or may not be connected to a personal deity. In this way, Hume foreshadowed Darwin's rejection of the argument from design. But despite these significant objections, within a few years of Hume's death, a book was published that gave the argument from design perhaps its most popular expression.

William Paley (1743–1805) published his *Natural Theology* in 1803, and it became a bestseller. Paley summarized discoveries in the natural sciences and presented them as proofs for the existence of a Creator God. The longer title for his book was *Evidence of the Existence and Attributes of the Deity, Collected from the Appearances of Nature.* In its first twenty years, every print-run sold out, and the book influenced an entire generation of academics. It was highly regarded by a young Charles Darwin who read it while a student in Cambridge – in the very room where William Paley had once worked. In his autobiography, Darwin claimed he could have written its main arguments out in full from memory.

Paley relied on the principle of analogy to argue from what we can see in the natural world to what this tells us about the existence of God. The basic analogy which underlies all his examples is this:

> In crossing a heath, suppose I pitched my foot against a stone, and were asked how the stone came to be there, I might possibly answer that, for any thing I knew to the contrary,

it had lain there for ever . . . But suppose I had found a
watch upon the ground, and it should be enquired how
the watch happened to be in that place, I should hardly think
of the answer which I had before given, that, for any thing
I knew, the watch might have always been there. Yet why
should not this answer serve for the watch, as well as for
the stone?[4]

The reason why we do not think that the watch can be treated
in the same way as the stone is that the watch shows a high
degree of complexity in the way its parts serve together a
common purpose. The 'watch must have had a maker'[5]
because the parts have been assembled according to a purpose
and function.

The first use Paley makes of this story is to consider the
complexity of the eye. Each component has been carefully
assembled to create an instrument far more sophisticated and
capable than a telescope. No-one suggests that a telescope
could be assembled by chance processes, so how the far more
complex eye could be explained without the guidance of a
designer is beyond reason. After the eye, Paley offers multiple
examples in order to make the same point. He considers
bones, muscles, insects and, in a slightly different way, the
findings of astronomy.

Paley presented his book not as a logical step-by-step
argument, but as a cumulative case for the Creator. The
examples build up a picture of complexity and design that
cannot be dismissed as the product of chance. The failure of
one example need not undermine the overall cumulative case.

Paley was aware of David Hume's objections to the argument from design. In particular, he engaged with the problem
of apparently poor design. What about disease, decay and
natural mechanisms that seem unnecessarily convoluted

for their purpose? An object may be designed and yet still malfunction:

> When we are enquiring simply after the existence of an intelligent Creator, imperfection, inaccuracy, liability to disorder, occasional irregularities, may subsist, in a considerable degree, without inducing any doubt into the question: just as a watch may frequently go wrong, seldom perhaps exactly right, may be faulty in some parts, defective in some, without the smallest ground of suspicion from thence arising, that it was not a watch; not made; or not made for the purpose ascribed to it.[6]

A faulty watch still provides evidence of design. The complexity of the components and their mutual dependence are evidence to us that it is a machine that someone has pieced together for a purpose. There may be other reasons why the watch may not be the best possible device for that function. Perhaps there is a compromise in the design that makes it small enough to carry. Perhaps there is a fault because over time moisture has crept into the components and caused damage. But faults and compromises in no way detract from our inference that the watch is the product of a watchmaker. David Hume's argument from apparent flaws was not decisive. Paley was a convincing and appealing writer, and his apologetic strategy was very successful in his time. So why do we not hear Paley's name so much today? Everything began to change in 1859 with the event we have already referred to: publication of *On the Origin of Species*.

Darwin and religion

Darwin had enthusiastically followed the work of William Paley's natural theology, but would depart from a key premise, and that would change everything. As a young man, Darwin describes the appeal of Paley in these terms: 'I did not at the time trouble myself about Paley's premises; and taking these on trust I was charmed and convinced by the long line of argumentation.'[7]

Animal life shows clear evidence of design and brilliant function. The species vary in their different environments so that they are better suited for the particular local challenges they face. In a sense, Darwin would also promote an argument from design. But while Paley had inferred a personal, creative Divine Being as the designer, Darwin would infer an impersonal, natural law as the designer: natural selection. The Divine Watchmaker of Paley's analogy was replaced by the blind watchmaker of Darwin, an analogy used by Richard Dawkins as the title of a more recent book on natural selection.

Like David Hume long before, Darwin stressed the cruelty of the natural world. The scale of death, decay and waste in natural selection is enormous. Further distressed by the loss of his ten-year-old daughter Annie in 1851, Darwin lost any faith in a good, loving God displaying himself through creation. The process of natural selection – heartless and cruel – seemed a more plausible explanation.

Did Darwin turn back to the God of the Bible and relinquish his theories on his deathbed? The story of a deathbed conversion has been retold so many times that it has passed into Christian folklore. Disentangling the fact from the fiction is almost impossible. Its origins are generally traced to a letter written in 1915 by Lady Hope to a newspaper. She claimed to have sat with Darwin as his health declined. One afternoon he declared his faith in Jesus and confessed of his theory: 'I was a young man with unformed ideas. I threw out queries, suggestions . . . People made a religion of them.'[8] Her account need not imply anything like a religious conversion on Darwin's part, but the story was so intriguing that it was rewritten, embellished and passed on through various forms of Christian preaching and apologetics.

James Moore has researched the story in great detail, and his conclusions are probably as much as we will ever know. The Lady Hope of the letter was an itinerant social worker and evangelist who probably did visit Darwin at his home during the last months of his life while she was involved in outreach work in his village. Darwin was impressed with the work of these evangelists among the farm labourers. Writing to a tent preacher who had asked for assistance, Darwin commented, 'We have never been able to reclaim a drunkard, but through your services I do not know that there is one drunkard left in the village.'[9] It is quite possible that Lady Hope did meet Darwin, but her recollection of the deathbed conversion is ambiguous at best and probably exaggerated.

However, Darwin was never an atheist. There was always a glimmer of interest in the possibility of God. During the last year of Darwin's life, the Duke of Argyll suggested that it was hard to contemplate the intricate workings of organisms without seeing them as the product of an Intelligent Designer. Darwin replied, 'Well, that often comes over me with over-whelming force; but at other times it seems to go away.'[10] The intuitive appeal of the argument from design remains a powerful force, despite the apparent success of Darwinian evolution to provide an alternative explanation.

The Christian response to Darwin

Many evangelicals endorsed evolution through natural selection as the means God used to design the diversity of life. B. B. Warfield famously defended the theory as compatible with the infallibility of the Bible.[11] As an apologetic strategy, this may seem appealing. However, there are increasing numbers of Christians who see a significant flaw in this uneasy peace. The general secular population is far from persuaded on one view of origins. The statistics show that even in the UK there remains massive scepticism in the general population regarding the theory of evolution.[12]

How should a Christian respond to these issues? James Sire gives some blunt advice: 'In general, I believe that in their witness to their Christian faith most Christians should never raise the issue of evolution. They should talk about it only if they cannot avoid doing so.'[13] Sire highlights that it is not the central issue in our presentation of the gospel. We can understand what Christ has done and come to personal faith without deciding which scientific theory best describes human origins. However, critics point out that the theory of evolution is not simply about biology, but about a philosophical worldview. The naturalistic assumptions of the Enlightenment are deeply contrary to Christian faith. As we have already seen, they presuppose that natural processes can explain all things. The Enlightenment worldview excludes the possibility of an argument from design to a supernatural cause. An important problem many apologists raise with evolution is not so much the scientific data per se, but the philosophical presuppositions that are being used to interpret the data. Is evolutionary theory a neutral observation of the facts or something more?

Though Charles Darwin was an agnostic, evolutionary theory has made it possible to understand the origins of life without reference to a Creator God. Richard Dawkins has been the most notable proponent of the claim that evolution through natural selection destroys the argument from design and allows him the comfort of being what he calls an 'intellectually fulfilled atheist'.[14] In one sense, everyone accepts that there is design in nature. The question is how this apparent design came about. The Christian sees it as the product of the intelligent guidance of God. The atheist claims design is only an illusion and in fact the product of random mutations constrained by the environment. Francis Crick, co-discoverer of DNA and opponent of the design argument, warned, 'Biologists must constantly keep in mind that what they see was not designed, but rather evolved.'[15]

It is one thing to claim that science can only deal with the observation of material reality, but quite another to claim that there is nothing more than material reality. This is a pure assumption and entirely at odds with the Christian faith. As Phillip Johnson puts it:

> Naturalistic evolutionary theory, as part of the grand metaphysical story of science, says that creation was by impersonal and unintelligent forces. The opposition between the biblical and naturalistic stories is fundamental, and neither side can compromise over it. To compromise is to surrender.[16]

Regardless of what we believe about how the book of Genesis should be interpreted, there is an important point here for apologetics. Even without any scientific training, a Christian is able to raise questions about the worldview behind natural selection and some of its assumptions.

If there is one thing that will often upset the Darwinian evolutionist, it is to point out that evolution is a theory and not a fact. For example, Ernst Mayr states:

> It is now actually misleading to refer to evolution as a theory, considering the massive evidence that has been discovered over the last 140 years documenting its existence. Evolution is no longer a theory, it is simply a fact.[17]

Is evolution a fact? Yes, say the proponents, because the evidence is now overwhelming. Dawkins claims, 'Evolution is a fact in the same sense as it is a fact that Paris is in the Northern Hemisphere.'[18] This claim is an intellectual sleight of hand. If by evolution we mean something simple like 'change over time', then everyone concedes that the evidence is there. But if by evolution we are using shorthand to mean Darwinian descent through modification of all living beings from a common ancestor, then the evidence is rather less compelling. And if by evolution we mean development through natural processes of time, and chance mutation that could not possibly be connected to the guidance of a Divine Hand, then this is conjecture, not fact. Even Dawkins grudgingly admits this distinction: 'It is no longer possible to dispute the fact of evolution,' he asserts, while adding, 'but it could still (just) be doubted that natural selection is its major driving force.'[19]

This theoretical framework is finding dissenters within the scientific and wider academic community. Evolutionary theory has itself been modified and subjected to criticism over time. In some cases, its most basic assumptions are being questioned, and not only by those who have a religious antipathy towards the theory.[20] The late David Stove, a philosopher of science with no sympathy for creationism, wrote, 'On the subject of our species, Darwinism is a mere festering mass of errors.'[21] Michael Denton wrote a very influential text in 1985, *Evolution: A Theory in Crisis*,[22] in which he outlined a number of reasons why as a secular scientist he found the theory to be wanting. These included problems in the fossil record and in the complexity of organic molecular structures. Denton remains an evolutionist, but one who is critical of its total explanatory power:

> One hundred and twenty years ago it was possible for a sceptic
> to be forgiving, to give Darwinism the benefit of the doubt

and to allow that perhaps future discoveries would eventually fill in the blanks that were so apparent in 1859. Such a position is far less tenable today.[23]

Natural selection predicts slow, gradual change in the development of life on earth. The fossil record provides little evidence for transitional forms or slow development, while one would expect this to be a common feature. Darwin's expectations were not being confirmed by the fossil record during his own lifetime. This led to a little-publicized difference between himself and his colleague, Thomas Huxley. Huxley saw the fossil record as indicating what is sometimes called 'evolution through jerks' (something that would re-emerge as Punctuated Equilibrium[24]). Darwin did not accept that conclusion. He had faith that later discoveries would prove the theory correct: evolution is always through slow, gradual change. This was at the heart of the theory of evolution through natural selection. There is no guiding hand that would speed up the process when necessary. Evolution could not be through 'jerks' if it was to fit with the theory. Critics point out that the fossil record still stubbornly refuses to confirm Darwinian theory, even after 150 years of research. Complex forms of life appear and disappear, but we fail to find the evidence for slow, progressive development, and in particular the smooth story of transitional forms as one species evolves into another. Those who defend the theory point out that fossils form only in rare circumstances, and that gaps reflect problems in the geological record, not gaps in evolutionary development.

The molecular record

Darwin did not know about genetics and the DNA information element of life. What were animals formed of? For

Darwin, it was a simple blob of organic material. We now know that the simple organic cell is itself a highly complex system.

DNA (deoxyribonucleic acid) is the basic information content of an organism's genetic material. The human genome is the entire collection of this DNA information used in the organic construction of a person. Encoded in our DNA are 3.1 billion letters of information. It has been calculated that to read this information out loud at three letters per second would take thirty-one years![25] What we call the simple cell is anything but simple. The cell is a highly complex multi-part machine for transmitting and replicating information that makes a supercomputer look like a simple classroom calculator!

Reviewing the problems in the evidence, biologist Michael Denton wrote,

> Is it really credible that random processes could have constructed a reality, the smallest element of which – a functional protein or gene – is complex beyond our own creative capacities, a reality which is the very antithesis of chance, which excels in every sense anything produced by the intelligence of man?[26]

Denton does not argue for the existence of God, only that there are predetermined pathways that evolution must follow. Mutations do not arise by chance, but through some unidentified property that enables an organism to direct its own development. Denton is willing to dissent from the majority view because the evidence is pointing elsewhere. A Christian is entitled to share this dissent, and argue that the evidence points not to predetermined pathways but to a divine intelligence.

Michael Behe is a molecular biologist who has done just this. He has argued that the molecular machinery forming the cell is irreducibly complex. Every cell contains a vast array of complex machinery carrying out the various biological processes necessary to life. These machines cannot be formed by a series of small steps. Using the illustration of a mousetrap, Behe argues that a molecular system has a number of components that must all be in place for it to work. Evolution requires that every tiny step must produce a useful system in its own right for it to be preserved. But molecular systems like the bacterial flagellum are themselves part of the basic building blocks for life. And these systems are themselves multicomponent and irreducibly complex. However, an evangelical scientist, Francis Collins, is wary of this claim. He points out that, even in the decade since the publication of Behe's landmark book, *Darwin's Black Box*, the possible steps in the creation of the bacterial flagellum have been identified. Collins is concerned that this line of reasoning simply identifies the hand of God in anything we don't yet understand. The danger is that once we do understand them, we no longer need God.

> Ultimately a 'God of the gaps' religion runs a huge risk of simply discrediting faith. We must not repeat this mistake in the current era. Intelligent Design fits into this discouraging tradition, and faces the same ultimate demise.[27]

Richard Dawkins concurs: 'The "information challenge" turns out to be none other than our old friend: "How could something as complex as an eye evolve?"'[28] Whether we are describing the eye or the cell or a fully formed mammal, there is a similar basic issue: how do you get the complex from the simple? However, the Intelligent Design movement has pressed the point that there is a unique issue in the case of

DNA. Information cannot grow in complexity without intelligent guidance. Whether it is computer code or a work of literature, information does not increase through chance mutation but through conscious planning. Chance mutation invariably leads to a loss of information content, not to a gain. Time and again, mutations that we witness in fruit flies or humans demonstrate this point. Mutation does not enhance, but degrades an organism. DNA provides a unique challenge to the idea that chance mutation can explain the development of new information. If a university dissertation suffered a little random mutation before submission, it would almost certainly be the poorer for it.

An inconclusive theory

These objections do not prove the existence of God or the reliability of the Bible. Their purpose is simply to point out the inconclusive nature of the theory of evolution. Natural selection remains a theory that is open to debate. In particular, it relies upon the assumption that natural laws are all that are required to explain the phenomenon of nature. Because this is an assumption, it is not proven by scientific evidence. It is entirely fair for the Christian to point out how the evidence suggests the plausibility of the existence of a Supernatural Intelligence. The charge that we are presenting a 'God of the gaps' is misguided. It is not in the areas where we are ignorant that we assume an act of God; it is in the areas where we have evidence that we can identify the work of God. Apologists present God as active in all of creation. In that sense, there is no ultimate difference between 'natural laws' and 'supernatural events' – all things depend on the action of God. The evidence of an abrupt fossil record and an irreducibly complex molecular structure are not gaps in what we know; they *are* what we know! And it is what we know that is seen as evidence for the existence of an Intelligent Designer. This is why the argument from design, far from diminishing in significance with new discoveries, continues to gain adherents. One of the areas of scientific progress that has led to the clearest revival of the argument from design is physics.

Creation and the Big Bang

A century ago, scientists and school teachers all assumed a steady state universe without beginning or end. Even Albert Einstein mistakenly modified his theory of general relativity so that this assumption was not undermined. The universe has always been and always will be.

Observations, particularly those of the astronomer Edwin Hubble, pointed towards a universe that was rapidly expanding. These observations eventually led to the theory that space and time began at a single point nearly 14 billion years ago, and has since been expanding to its present size. Many discoveries were taken to confirm this idea, including the background microwave radiation of the universe. We used to glimpse this as a snowy fuzz on TV sets that had to be tuned to find a station, though nowadays digital TV sets have done away with that privilege. The pattern of the background radiation throughout the universe fits exactly what is expected of an explosion. The idea of an expanding universe had the inevitable implication that the expansion began at a single point. The term 'Big Bang' was coined by an astronomer, Fred Hoyle, to describe his own disquiet with a theory for which he had no enthusiasm. The concept of a moment from which all space and time began sounded too much like the Christian account of creation. Robert Jastrow (1925–2008), a director of the Mount Wilson Observatory and an influential member of NASA, describes the unease of many astronomers and scientists in discovering that the evidence points to creation:

> For the scientist who has lived by his faith in the power of reason, the story ends like a bad dream. He has scaled the mountains of ignorance; he is about to conquer the highest peak; as he pulls himself over the final rock, he is greeted by a band of theologians who have been sitting there for centuries.[29]

You can be sure that secular thought would prefer some form of steady state or eternal universe rather than the Big Bang. Indeed, outside of those religions influenced by the Genesis account, there is no real parallel to the doctrine of creation out of nothing. The Eastern religions, much Greek philosophy and Ancient Near Eastern religions assume matter to be eternal:

> It is unfortunate that some people oppose the Big Bang theory out of the feeling that it implies randomness in creation, because nothing could be further from the truth. Perhaps the name leads people to the wrong picture, of a chaotic explosion. On the contrary, modern science has shown that incredible balances and tuning were involved in the Big Bang, with precisions on the order of one part in 10^{100}.[30]

The 'balances' and 'tuning' of the universe refer to the various laws which were there at the beginning of space and time, but could have been different. Rodney Holder, astrophysicist and Fellow of the Royal Astronomical Society, likens the accuracy of these initial conditions to firing a gun from one end of the universe to the other (a distance of ten billion light years) and hitting a coin.[31] Our universe is incredibly unlikely. But not only is our universe unlikely in its complexity, stability and ability to sustain intelligent life, it also gives rise to the obvious question: what caused the Big Bang? That's a question that makes many intellectuals uncomfortable. Fred Hoyle, the non-Christian astronomer, saw these implications in his now famous words: 'A common-sense interpretation of the facts suggests that a superintellect has monkeyed with the physics, as well as with the chemistry and biology, and that there are no blind forces worth speaking about in nature.'

The Kalam cosmological argument

Kalam is an Arabic word meaning 'speech', and describes a particular form of the cosmological argument that developed among Islamic philosophers. William Lane Craig has given a detailed presentation and defence of this argument which he draws from the work of an Islamic theologian, Al-Ghazali (c. 1055–1111).[32] Unlike other versions of the cosmological argument, this one is based on the universe having a beginning. The reason why it was found first among Muslim theologians is that they had continued a keen interest in Aristotle who had been neglected in the Christian West. Aristotle would have been unsurprised by evidence pointing to a big bang – he had already proposed reasons why the universe must have had a beginning.

The argument works like this. Whatever begins to exist has a cause. The universe began to exist. Therefore the universe has a cause. This apparently simple argument is profound in its implications for science and theology. The Kalam cosmo-logical argument fits well with the Genesis account of creation, and finds experimental confirmation in the evidence for the Big Bang. Regardless of what Christians believe about the age of the universe or the origins of the human race, we all agree that there was a moment of creation at which the matter of the universe began to exist. This fact needs a causal explanation. Who or what caused the universe to come into existence?

William Lane Craig's detailed defence of the argument includes close consideration of the many objections that may be made to its premises. For example, why couldn't the universe just be infinite in age, without beginning or end? This was assumed in the steady state model of the universe. Craig points out how muddled we get when we start describing the universe as infinite. While infinite is a useful word in mathematics, it is a complicated word to apply to real situations. Imagine a trail of upright dominos set up in a row so that as each one falls it knocks another one over. If the domino standing where you are falls because of the domino falling before it, and the dominos stretch back into infinite time past, then how could the present domino fall? A stretch of a thousand dominos might take twenty minutes to fall before they reached you. A stretch of 10,000 dominos might take a little over three hours to reach you. But an infinitely long stretch of dominos would need an infinite stretch of time to reach you, and that is the same as saying they never would. And why would the domino before you fall today rather than have fallen yesterday or a long time ago? If the universe has always been here, then how could we ever have reached 'today'? If we cannot ever reach the point of infinity in the future, then how could we ever have reached it in the past? A universe that has always existed is deeply problematic. In fact, philosophically it is unclear that it is a meaningful statement. While it is possible to say that the universe will always exist into the future (though contemporary theories cast doubt on that possibility too!), it is not possible to say that the universe has always existed in the past. To describe our universe as of infinite duration from the past is to deny that there could ever be a present. It would take an infinity of time to reach today – and nothing can have been around that long!

Another objection is to deny that whatever begins to exist must have a cause. Haven't we all seen a magician pull a rabbit out of a hat? Couldn't something pop out of nowhere? For example, Stephen Hawking denies that the universe itself needs any prior or greater explanation for its existence:

> Spontaneous creation is the reason there is something rather than nothing, why the universe exists, why we exist. It is not necessary to invoke God to light the blue touch paper and set the universe going.[33]

What does Hawking mean by 'spontaneous creation'? Perhaps there is simply something that begins uncaused in at least this one situation. But why would one think this? In every area of life, we assume that things always have a cause. In fact, science proceeds on the assumption that every event or reaction we see has a cause. Now why would the beginning of everything be the one exception to the rule? Surely it would be better to concede there is a cause, and if we're an unbeliever try to find a non-divine cause? Actually, Hawking does try to offer more of an explanation – he suggests that it is because of the law of gravity that spontaneous creation can arise. As John Lennox comments, 'By Hawking's own argument the question has merely been deflected to: who created the law of gravity? And this is a question that he does not answer.'[34] Hawking is entitled to identify a different cause to that offered by Christians, but his attempt to state 'spontaneous creation' suggests smoke and mirrors.

Sometimes people try to turn this point back against the existence of God. For example, if everything that begins to exist must have a cause, then can't we ask the question: 'What caused God?', and if we can ask that question, are we not then locked into an infinite regress of cause and effect with various beings required to create further creators? This response commits the ambiguity fallacy. We are only describing things that begin to exist (like people, stars and the universe), not something without a beginning (like God). No orthodox Christian describes God as having a beginning, so there is no reason to look for a cause. Notice that Craig's carefully worded Kalam argument used the statement: 'whatever begins to exist has a cause' – God is not one of those things.

A similar objection is that Christians happily describe God as infinite, and so should not object to the possibility that the universe is infinite. It comes as some surprise for many Christians to realize that theologians do not generally describe God as infinite. In biblical language, it is better to describe God as eternal, because he exists outside of time. Time is one of his many creations. So God is eternal, rather than infinite, being outside of space and time which are his creations. This is why philosophers call God 'timeless'. To describe God as infinite is misleading, because it gives the impression that God is within time.

Avoiding creation

Sometimes scientists suggest modified versions of the Big Bang – including an oscillating universe or a multiverse. In an oscillating universe those universes have come and gone, as matter expands and contracts over and over again. This suggestion has many critical objections from within the scientific community, but even if it were true it would still rely on some initial creation of time and space. Even a series of many universes cannot go back into an infinite past. The observational and theoretical evidence still points to an initial moment of creation. To draw on the speculative image of an oscillating universe as a way of sidestepping the problem of creation has an air of desperation.

However, not only is the starting point of creation a pointer to the existence of a Creator, the nature of the universe that resulted tells us even more. The high-precision laws that govern our universe are not only highly unlikely; they are practically the only laws that would permit the development of intelligent life.

This is called the fine-tuning of the universe. The universe is governed by various forces and ratios, including the strength of gravity, the strong nuclear force which binds atomic particles together and the electromagnetic force. All of these have certain values which seem to be arbitrary. They could have been slightly stronger or slightly weaker. Or they could have been wildly different. Like driving a car along the road, there is a huge range of possible speeds at which we might travel – even keeping within the national law (and that law in turn could have been set differently). Now the point scientists make is that if any of these various forces or ratios had been slightly different, there would have been no life. A slight change in any of these forces would have massive effects on the rest of the universe. Instead of bonding together, atoms would tear apart; instead of fusing as stars and generating carbon, they would have at best been in constant chaotic flux.

These are the precision factors that Holder referred to in his illustration of a gun firing a bullet over a vast distance and hitting a bullseye. There are many similar illustrations, all of which convey the point that the odds of such an arrangement coming about by chance are astronomically small. The existence of an Intelligent Designer is far more plausible.

Sometimes it is suggested that there is nothing unique about our universe – every possible universe with every possible variation in the forces and laws would be unique in its own way. But this suggestion misses the point. There is only one, very precise, finely tuned set of forces that would provide a stable universe where atoms can form and combine and remain that way for long periods of time. It is this stability which is unique and which is essential to the formation of complex things like living organisms. The other possible universes might each be unique in their own way, but they would almost all share the characteristic of not being life-sustaining.

A related objection to the fine-tuning argument also uses the multiverse theory. This theory asks us to imagine that our universe is only one of possibly infinite universes that may appear like bubbles out of nothing. Given so many, it is not surprising that one would have appeared able to support complex life. And given that we are complex organisms, it is inevitable that we are part of this particular universe. This objection works well because, if the odds against the initial conditions of our universe are one in 10 billion times 123, that becomes less astounding if there actually are 10 billion times 123 universes!

As an objection, the multiverse theory is fatally flawed. It is built on pure assumption, and the only motivation for adopting it is the antipathy to the obvious alternative: that the universe is the product of Intelligent Design. It seems to be a deliberate invention to avoid the obvious conclusion that our universe is incredibly improbable. There are further problems with the theory, even among those who do not use it to make this objection. The idea of a multiverse itself requires some kind of energy or force to bring universes into existence. This force or energy requires explaining: where did this force come from anyway? So the multiverse theory just seems to be a deliberate attempt to avoid the conclusion and is itself susceptible to explanatory problems. As Paul Davies points out,

> Perhaps future developments in science will lead to more direct evidence for other universes, but until then, the seemingly miraculous concurrence of numerical values that nature has assigned to her fundamental constants must remain the most compelling evidence for an element of cosmic design.[35]

Science and progress

Of course, in sharing our faith we need to be careful about our use of current scientific theories. Commitment to Christianity is not undermined by present scientific theories, but neither does it require them. To try to prove the existence of God from current theories is to risk looking foolish if those theories change. C. S. Lewis gave wise advice:

> Sentences beginning 'science has now proved' should be avoided. If we try to base our apologetic on some recent development in science, we shall usually find that just as we have put the finishing touches to our argument, science has changed its mind and quietly withdrawn the theory we have been using as our foundation stone.[36]

We can show that Christianity is compatible with the same data that scientists use. We can indicate the role that Christians have played in the formation and development of contemporary Western science. We can also unmask philosophical theories that frame the data in a materialist view of the universe. For example, Christians may well recognize the genius of Charles Darwin in identifying the limited role of natural selection in adaptation among species, without needing to subscribe to the grand Darwinian view that natural selection explains the development of all complex life. After a robust response to Dawkins' arguments, David Robertson wisely notes,

> I think it is very foolish for Christians or others to seek to prove or disprove God on the basis of a current scientific theory or on empirical evidence alone. But science within its own constraints as the observation of what God has made is a marvelous and often faith-affirming thing.[37]

The design argument has always been one of the most popular defences of the Christian faith. Scientific developments over the twentieth century continued to provide reason to use a design argument. Antony Flew, a long-time atheist philosopher, changed his mind late in life through these developments: 'It now seems to me that the findings of more than fifty years of DNA research have provided materials for a new and enormously powerful argument to design.'[38] The use of hard evidence to argue the case for design often needs more specialized training. But all Christians are able to present the intuitive case that this world speaks of the existence of God. The intuition that the universe is a beautiful, awesome gift runs very deep in our psychology. Our place within the universe as self-conscious organisms, aware of moral claims upon our lives and a desire to know the truth, makes us astoundingly unlikely in an otherwise harsh environment.

So is this all mere luck? Are we the product of a great, natural fluke? Or are we the result of God's planning and purpose? The answer to this question is not settled simply by appeal to scientific data.

9. Dealing with diversity

*The most pressing question on the problem
of faith is whether a man as a civilized
being can believe in the divinity of the Son
of God, Jesus Christ, for therein rests the
whole of our faith.*
Fyodor Dostoevsky

What about other world religions?

This is a question of great contemporary importance. It has
been remarked that, for much of the history of Christian
thought, apologetics dealt with issues as if there were only
Christians, Jews and Muslims. Since globalization and the
spread of communication networks, this parochial view of
intellectual thought is entirely out of date. The defence of Christianity needs to recognize a multiplicity of religious options.

So why are there so many religions? The Bible leads us to
expect this state of affairs. The Old Testament world assumes
the existence of many 'gods' (though the Old Testament itself
acknowledges only one true God, e.g. Deuteronomy 6:4). The
New Testament is set in a thoroughly multicultural Roman
Empire where the gods of Greece, Rome, Egypt and Arabia
vied for attention. The reason for this diversity is explained by
the Bible writers. God has created all people in his own image.

He has given a general revelation of himself which is accessible to all people (Romans 1:18–32). There is good reason to think that we can expect some Christian doctrines to be acknowledged and supported by the adherents of other religions. However, a natural leaning towards idolatry causes this revelation to be distorted and forgotten.

A key question that the very existence of world religions raises for Christians is the perceived narrowness. Can we claim that God has revealed himself in an exclusive way through the life of Jesus? This objection had been made throughout the Enlightenment Age. Charles Darwin wrote in his autobiography,

> At the present day the most usual argument for the existence of an intelligent God is drawn from the deep inward conviction and feelings which are experienced by most persons. But it cannot be doubted that Hindoos, Mahomadans and others might argue in the same manner and with equal force in favour of the existence of one God, or of many Gods, or as with Buddhists of no God.[1]

As global trade, exploration and understanding grew, so did the question: Is Christianity really so unique?

Pluralism

We start with a slippery word. Pluralism can simply be a factual description of contemporary society. We live in a pluralist or multicultural society. Particularly in the last few decades, Western Europe and America have become religiously diverse. In this sense, pluralism is simply a descriptive word. However, it can also carry a more prescriptive sense of what we are supposed to believe.

As a prescription, pluralism is a theory about the relation-ship between religions. At a popular level, it is the view of those who hold that all the major world religions are responses to the same God. Sometimes this idea is illustrated by using a very old parable of ten blind men and an elephant. The story goes that a king ordered an elephant to be brought into his courtyard and had the blind men describe what they could feel with their limited senses. One touched the tusk and thought it a spear; another held the tail and described it as a snake. In this way, there were ten different descriptions of the same elephant. Analogously, the world religions are different descriptions of the same ultimate reality. The differences arise because human beings have limited senses and cannot grasp the whole. So rather than argue about who has the correct picture of God, we should humbly accept that we have all grasped a facet of something much greater. This parable was originally told by the Buddha, but, as we shall see, his telling included an important twist which is missing from this popular version!

John Hick (1922 –) was a very influential philosopher of religion during the twentieth century. In the course of his work, he has come to promote what he calls a pluralist inter-pretation of religion. His first statement of religious pluralism was found in his 1973 publication: *God and the Universe of Faiths*.

Instead of seeing Christ as the centre of faith, we should see that even Christ was directing us to a Divine Being beyond all human language. Hick's argument was that, if we under-stand God rather than Christ to be at the centre of faith, then we can accept that all religions are responding in some way to the same God, regardless of what they think of Christ. This was a temporary suggestion. Even the word 'God' remains a particular description of this being. Some religions – such as

Buddhism – have no place for an ultimate, personal God. Therefore, in later writings Hick dispensed with the loaded term 'God' in favour of the more neutral term 'ultimate reality' or the 'real'. Because this thing is strictly beyond direct human knowledge, we can only describe it in philosophical categories that would be compatible with any religious outlook. Hick refers to the real as 'he/she/it' to avoid any gender bias.

There is a heavy price to pay for this pluralist reinterpretation. In order to claim that every major religion is valid, we must also argue that they are all invalid. Rather than leading to the claim that all religions are equally true, we are led to conclude that all religions are equally mistaken – though they all, accidentally, offer a pathway to a genuine experience. It could be argued that pluralism is an example of 'begging the question'. It already assumes that all religions are responding to the same Ultimate Reality, and then interprets all the evidence in the light of this assumption. Hick offers this account as an 'interpretation' of religion. Pluralism is not supposed to be a religion in itself, only a framework in which to make sense of religion. But as a framework, it functions more like the legendary Procrustean bed. Procustes made a bed perfect in size for any visitor – those too short were stretched to fit, those too tall were cut down to size. Truth claims and historical events that do not fit the grand universal theme are lopped off. General ethical themes or the more vague mystical traditions of religion are stretched to become the most important part of any faith.

So what about the parable of the blind men and the elephant? Isn't this a wise, ancient tale indicating our need humbly to admit our ignorance and accept that apparently quite different religious perspectives might all have their own outlook on the one truth? The fly in the ointment of this interpretation is that it misses a crucial point that the Buddha was making. The question is: who is in the position of the king? Who is able to make this judgment on the partial, limited understandings of the poor blind men? The king represents the enlightened one. He has the clear vision. He can see what the blind men cannot see. Likewise, the pluralist claims a perspective on the world religions, hidden to their devotees.

In contrast to the pluralist agenda, Christians should defend the uniqueness of Jesus Christ and salvation. 'Uniqueness' is a word that needs to be clarified. In one sense, every person is unique. It is a trivial statement to describe a religion as unique. Your fingerprint is unique. There is nothing unique about being unique! What matters is not that Christianity is unique, but that its central message is uniquely true and uniquely universal. It is the truth that, at best, other claims can only shadow it, and it is universally relevant to every person.

The uniqueness of Scripture

Most religions revere books as scripture. Hindus revere the Vedas, Muslims the Qur'an, Jews the Torah. This gives rise to the vague idea that scriptures are all the same kind of thing. In fact, Wilfred Cantwell Smith, Professor of Comparative Religion and director of Harvard's Center for the Study of Religion, attempted to define scripture in a way compatible with all, but concluded an exhaustive study by remarking:

> The term 'scripture' was, after all, Western, naming not a
> basic human category but constituting a Western one. It was
> recently summoned into service to interpret data from the rest
> of the world that at first blush appeared roughly similar; but
> these have proven on inquiry to be considerably less similar
> than had been imagined.[2]

There is no such thing as 'scripture', only different texts that religions revere for varied reasons. The Christian under-standing of Scripture is subtly distinct from the claims made by the followers of other religions for their sacred texts.

The Bible is a library of books rather than a single volume. It is a record of God's saving acts and spoken words delivered through history. Over forty different authors writing on three different continents in at least two different languages contrib-uted to Scripture. As such, one might expect the Bible to be a contradictory collection of unrelated ideas. Instead, we find a collection of great harmony recording a single story of salvation history from creation to the age of Christianity. We find a common Hebrew worldview emerging from these varied texts. Prophecies focus on the person and work of the Messiah who is revealed to be the son of Joseph, born in Bethlehem.

How does the Bible compare with other scriptures? This kind of comparison is helpful because we can draw attention more clearly to what makes the Christian view unique. The Bhagavad Gita is one of the great collections of texts treated as scripture by the various Hindu traditions. They are beautiful poetic songs and romantic stories that form a collective mythology. Nowhere do they offer any claim to be historical records. They are mythic poetry offering spiritual truths or insights. In that sense, they would compare better with John Bunyan's *Pilgrim's Progress* than with the Bible. Bunyan's famous work is a spiritual allegory rather than a historical work. It lays no claim to being rooted in time and space.

Far removed from the poetic scriptures of ancient Hinduism is the rather more recent collection known to us as the Qur'an. These are a collection of chapters (Surahs) which record visions given to Mohammed by the angel Gabriel over a period of twenty-three years. They are not historical records. They lay no claim to being eyewitness accounts. According to Muslim tradition, the personality of Mohammed is not supposed to have had any significant bearing on the text. The Muslim claim is that the Arabic words are exactly as written in heaven. Therefore, it is not strictly possible even to translate the Qur'an. A translation is called a 'commentary'. The authority and authenticity of the Qur'an rely entirely on the trustworthiness of Mohammed. Because they are not records from the times of Abraham, Moses, David or Jesus, but were written much later, they do not provide us with first-hand access to the events described.

Interestingly, the Qur'an itself is not critical of the Jewish and Christian Scriptures. It speaks positively of these books (for example, Surah 4:162–163; 10:94–95; 29:46). However, the content of the Qur'an contradicts what we read in the Bible. Of particular importance is the description of Jesus. The Qur'an describes Jesus as a prophet, not as God incarnate, and denies that he suffered the humiliation of death by crucifixion. Therefore, according to Islamic tradition, the Gospels have now been tampered with and are not the books commended by Mohammed. This is particularly significant because, whatever arguments are made about the form of the Gospels in the first century, we have no reason to doubt the clear contents of the Gospels by the fifth and sixth centuries when the Qur'an was written. Therefore, in order to establish what happened in first-century Jerusalem, the records of the New Testament are a far more obvious place to start than revelations supposedly given directly 600 years later in a different part of the world.

Whether we are considering the ancient spiritual poetry of the Hindu Vedas or the later visionary writings of Mohammed, there is no need for Christians to ridicule other writings. In some circumstances, showing historical inaccuracies or problems in transmission can undermine their claim to special revelation. However, in many conversations, this kind of criticism can be seen as offensive or distasteful. Instead, we can simply draw attention to the ways in which the Bible is different from these other books. In fact, the Christian doctrine of revelation is not ultimately focused on the book itself, but on the person about whom the book speaks. God has revealed himself through Jesus Christ, and it is to him that the Scriptures lead.

For the purposes of apologetics, we do not need to establish that the Bible is inerrant, only that it is historically reliable. The inerrancy of Scripture is the teaching that the Bible is without error in every matter it addresses. There are no mistakes in the moral and spiritual teaching it gives, nor in the historical and scientific claims that it makes. To demonstrate an error, whether moral or factual, is to undermine the inerrancy of the Bible. However, defending the Bible from claimed errors can become a distraction in evangelism. We do not have enough days left in our lives to test every possible objection to the claims about Scripture. Proving that the Bible is inerrant or infallible is impossible. Christians believe that the Bible is without error because Jesus taught that the Bible is infallible. Our friends will probably not accept that the Bible is infallible or inerrant until they first put their faith in Jesus as Lord and God. So our task is more modest: to demonstrate the reliability of the New Testament as a witness to the identity of Jesus.

When was the New Testament written?

Unlike earlier Hindu poetic literature or later Islamic visionary writings, the New Testament is a careful record of historical events from the time of Jesus. Some accounts are eyewitness (John 1:14; Acts 2:32; 1 Corinthians 15:3–8; 2 Peter 1:16), while others draw upon those eyewitness claims:

> Many have undertaken to draw up an account of the things
> that have been fulfilled among us, just as they were handed
> down to us by those who from the first were eye-witnesses and
> servants of the word.
> (Luke 1:1–2; see also Hebrews 2:3)

Of course the reason for scepticism regarding the New Testament is the accounts of supernatural events that cluster around the life of Jesus. His virgin birth, his miracles, the empty tomb, the resurrection appearances and the supernatural healings associated with the work of the Holy Spirit are hard for many people to believe. However, if the New Testament writings are sober and thoughtful in all the areas that we can test – such as matters of history – then we are invited to trust these accounts in areas which we cannot test directly. This is why we can limit our apologetic case to explaining the reliability of the New Testament.

Dan Brown's best-selling *The Da Vinci Code* makes an unsettling claim regarding the New Testament. One of his characters, the historian Sir Leigh Teabing, claims,

> Some of the gospels that Constantine attempted to eradicate
> managed to survive. The Dead Sea Scrolls were found in the
> 1950s hidden in a cave near Qumran in the Judean desert.
> And, of course, the Coptic Scrolls in 1945 at Nag Hammadi
> . . . The scrolls highlight glaring historical discrepancies and
> fabrications, clearly confirming that the modern Bible was
> compiled and edited by men who possessed a political agenda.[3]

These words are riddled with errors, but reflect the very general impression many people have about the New Testament. So the Gospels are the unreliable product of a later political agenda. Such a claim is far removed from the truth.

What are the earliest records of the life of Jesus? One might immediately think they are the four Gospels of the New Testament, but this is not true. Some of the New Testament letters are probably earlier, and these contain references to earlier writings still. Paul was executed under Emperor Nero in AD 64. This means that all his letters must predate AD 64. The earliest letters are probably those to the Thessalonians, Corinthians and Galatians, which all date to the early 50s AD. This would mean that they were written within twenty years of the death of Jesus. Furthermore, the letters themselves refer to information already well known among the early Christians. It is possible to reconstruct the main features of the birth, life, teaching, death and resurrection of Jesus from these references. They don't present the material in the way the Gospels will, but they already assume familiarity with this story. In his study of the historical basis for our understanding of Jesus, Paul Barnett makes this point:

> Paul's earliest letters, but also James, 1 Peter and Hebrews,
> reflect the fact that the readers and their churches had
> become believers because of the proclamation of the gospel.
> At the same time these letters reflect a knowledge of the
> historical Jesus to which the writer can appeal, and which
> the readers share.[4]

These letters also bear references to traditions, sayings and writings already in circulation among the early Christians. Therefore, these citations must themselves be earlier traditions than the letters in which we find them. Given their poetic structure, examples might include Philippians 2:5–11 and Colossians 1:15–20, along with the creedal statement of 1 Corinthians 15:1–4. These examples demonstrate that the earliest teachings of the New Testament affirm a very high view of Jesus as the pre-existent Son of God, who died for sin and rose again from the dead. These ideas are not later developments owed to convoluted theological reflection. They are the bedrock understanding of Jesus, upon which later thinkers would reflect.

Dating the Gospels

Of course the Gospels themselves: Matthew, Mark, Luke and John, provide the most direct and complete description of the life and teaching of Jesus. How early are these documents? The earliest complete New Testament manuscripts are the *Codex Vaticanus* and the *Codex Sinaiticus,* dating to the fourth century. Writings from the ancient world did not tend to survive well, as we've seen, apart from in the dry desert conditions of Egypt or the Dead Sea region. Given that these areas were not highly populated, it should not surprise us that we do not have complete manuscripts from earlier than this. However, there are a vast number of manuscript fragments from the second and third centuries. A fragment of John 18:31–33 and 18:37–38 is the earliest manuscript accepted by all scholars. Found in Egypt, this is called the John Rylands fragment or P46 and may date to as early as AD 125.[5] As a copy of other copies, it indicates that the original text must have been written much earlier still. This is particularly interesting because the Gospel of John is generally thought to be a later Gospel on account of its reflective theological style of writing. Another very early manuscript is composed of fragments of Matthew 26:7–33, which may even date to the first century. Apart from these direct remains of the New Testament, there are also a vast number of citations from the Gospels and other New Testament books found among other early writings. For example, all four Gospels are cited in letters and sermons written by Polycarp and Ignatius around AD 110. From sources like these, we can indirectly put together the contents of our New Testament.

The four Gospel accounts all claim to have arisen from among the first generation of Christians, and they indicate a dependence on eyewitness material. There is also material shared among what are called the 'Synoptic Gospels': Matthew, Mark and Luke. In itself, this is hardly surprising. The Gospels all concern the same historical figure, and so it is no surprise that they share common material. However, the similarities extend in places to the exact same Greek wording. This is persuasive evidence that some kind of relationship existed between Matthew, Mark and Luke. The most influential explanation is that there was a fourth body of material labelled Q (short for a German word, *Quelle*, meaning 'source').

This hypothesis has led to enormous confusion at a popular level. For example, the atheist Christopher Hitchens makes this claim:

> The book on which all four [Gospels] may possibly have been based, known speculatively to scholars as 'Q', has been lost forever, which seems distinctly careless on the part of the god who is claimed to have 'inspired' it.[6]

This description is wrong at so many levels. No-one claims all four Gospels are based upon 'it' – only that there is evidence that three of the Gospels have some shared material. No-one claims 'it' was a single book. Q is not an actual text, but a hypothesis that another group of texts existed and were shared between at least two of the Gospels in the Bible. Furthermore, no-one claims 'it' was inspired. There is nothing disturbing about the suggestion that collections of the teachings and actions of Jesus were in circulation from the very beginning of the church. Indeed, Luke indicates his own dependence on other writings and might have been referring to some of these accounts in Luke 1:1–3.

An interesting argument for dating the Gospels very early comes from an unlikely quarter. John A. T. Robinson was a theologian deeply sceptical of Christianity's supernatural claims. However, as a New Testament scholar, he was persuaded that all the four Gospels date to before AD 70.[7] This is a key date in Jewish-Christian history because it was the year when Rome launched a particularly savage attack on an uprising of the population of Jerusalem and destroyed the great Herodian temple. Remains of the violent damage done by the Romans can still be seen in Jerusalem today in the archaeological excavation around the south-west corner of the Temple Mount. The destruction of the temple brought the entire priestly sacrificial system to an end and set the scene for later rabbinical Judaism. In the future, Judaism would focus on the synagogue not the temple, and the laws of purity rather than sacrifice.

The destruction of the temple was of profound significance for Jewish self-understanding, and marks a watershed in Jewish history. In the light of this significant event, the New Testament should be understood as belonging to the era pre-AD 70. What little reference there is to the destruction of the temple belongs to prophecy and apocalyptic. In general, the Gospels certainly assume that the temple is still standing. Judaism continues to focus on the priestly sacrificial system. The geographical and political references around Jerusalem all assume the readers understood the arrangements prior to the destruction of the temple. Within a generation, it would have become necessary to explain the activities and locations of the various temple areas. In the light of this material, among other observations, Robinson makes the unusual step of affirming an early date for the Gospel of John, prior to AD 70.[8]

The right stuff

The canon of the New Testament refers to the measure of which books belong and which should be excluded. The canon was debated over the two centuries following the resurrection of Jesus. This led to the inaccurate claim that the canon was not decided until two North African councils, one in Hippo (AD 393) and one in Carthage (AD 397). The fact is that the agreed canon of the New Testament emerged voluntarily as churches gradually shared texts in the century following the death of the apostles.

We can make this case by pointing out that the canon of the New Testament was being recognized earlier in church history. It is true that some of the books of the New Testament were disputed and debated, chief among them James, Jude, 2 Peter, 2 and 3 John and other additional books such as the Shepherd of Hermas.[9] But this dispute demonstrates that the early church was aware of the need for some kind of criteria. The church shared the same concerns we have today with authenticity and apostolic authority.

The four Gospels were accepted as authentic very early in church history. One of the earliest lists of New Testament books is called the 'Muratorian Fragment' which dates to AD 180–200. Along with most of the letters, Acts and Revelation, it includes the four Gospels. Being fragmentary, it is incomplete. Luke and John are cited by name, but Matthew and Mark are not. However, Luke is referred to as the third Gospel, leaving little doubt that the four Gospels were all part of the original list. In AD 170, a Christian called Tatian harmonized the four Gospels we have into a single flowing narrative called the *Diatessaron*. Even earlier in church history we find the four Gospels cited by other authors, and from them we can reconstruct how the New Testament looked at that time.

Excluded books

Related to canon is the issue of spurious or non-canonical Gospels. Dan Brown makes reference to these in his novel. There are many of these Gospels in circulation, including the Gospel of Thomas, the Gospel of Mary, the Gospel of Judas and the Gospel of Barnabas. Are we being selective in our choice? The simple answer is that we are, but with very good reason. It is hardly surprising that later, fanciful accounts of Jesus would emerge, given his significance for the early believers.[10]

The Nag Hammadi collection of writings is a primary source for these alternative traditions. The character of Teabing in *The Da Vinci Code* makes reference to them and even suggests that they are more accurate sources for the life of Jesus than the New Testament itself. This is pure fiction. Nag Hammadi refers to the location in Egypt where these documents were found in 1945. They were a collection of thirteen books considered heretical in the fifth century. The fact that not a single canonical book from the Old or New Testament is found among them suggests that they were deliberately buried as a collection of non-canonical texts. The jars in which they were found date to the fifth century, indicating the time of their burial. The documents all share a Gnostic perspective. Gnosticism was a later second-century movement that fused Christian imagery with Greek philosophical ideas. The Gnostic Gospels, including the Gospel of Truth and the Gospel of Philip, are much later than the New Testament.

Anyone who takes the trouble to read these first-hand will immediately be struck by how different they are from the biblical texts. They do not report the same historical or geographical concerns. Nor are they sympathetic to the Jewish Hebrew worldview of the Old Testament. For example, they deny the goodness of the material creation and place emphasis on a non-material spiritual realm. This kind of distinction is alien to the first-century Jewish and Christian writers of the New Testament. For reasons like these, the Gnostic movement is seen as a later development and is rightly rejected by the early church as heretical. As a source of information on the historical Jesus, these Gospels are of little worth.[11]

In putting this evidence together, we can state unequivocally that the New Testament is a reliable historical record dating from the first generation of believers. Sceptics may want to doubt its contents, reject the claims of Jesus or question its coherence, but there is no basis on which to deny its essential historicity. With this fact established, we have a unique historic window into the life of a man who has had the single most significant impact on human history.

The uniqueness of Jesus

Most religions have a place of admiration for Jesus. The Eastern religions recognize him as a guru. There is even a far-fetched idea that Jesus travelled eastwards during the unknown years of his youth and studied some form of Buddhism. He was an 'enlightened' one like the Buddha on his return to Palestine. Muslims recognize Jesus as a prophet. Early Jewish traditions were fiercely critical of Jesus, but more contemporary Jewish thinkers have been more positive, particularly as Christian theologians have emphasized the Jewishness of Jesus.

When the Monty Python team prepared to write a parody of the life of Jesus, they found that they couldn't quite produce the film that they had intended. The resulting *Life of Brian* made fun of a parallel life to that of Jesus. John Cleese explained, 'The moment you got really near the figure of Christ, it just wasn't really funny because Christ was wise and flexible and intelligent and he didn't have any of the things that comedy is about – envy, greed, malice, avarice, lust, stupidity.'[12] Apart from revealing a somewhat limited view of comedy, this reflection admits that when we encounter the character of Christ in the Gospels first-hand, most people are confronted by someone who commands our attention and admiration. But the impact of Jesus cannot be explained solely by his teachings, most of which were not unique to him.

Dead man walking

Jesus rose from the dead. This is the claim that everything turns upon. The resurrection was not merely Jesus' survival through a near-death experience or even a resuscitation after death. Those would be remarkable but not exceptional. The resurrection of Jesus is the restoration and transformation of his body and personality after his death and burial. It is a bodily resurrection, but it is also a transformation of the body. Jesus did not rise from the dead like the son of the widow of Nain, or Lazarus, both of whom would later die natural deaths. The resurrection of Jesus was a first glimpse into the new creation which his teaching on the kingdom proclaimed. If Jesus rose from the dead, then we are right to take his teachings seriously. We have reason to trust him and to live this life in the light of an eternal life beyond the grave. It is clear that in the preaching and teaching of the early Christians, the resurrection loomed large. It gave them confidence, and many of them had been eyewitnesses of the greatest event of human history. Among early Christian apologists too, the fact of the resurrection loomed large.

The historical credentials for the resurrection are very strong, and they need to be because the claim is so significant. Various objections are laid at the claim that Jesus rose from the dead. Most imply that it was his impact that gave rise to some kind of resurrection experience. To respond to this objection, we first need to establish that this is not what the New Testament teaches, but that the New Testament presents an eyewitness memory that must be taken seriously. This is why our discussion of the first-century character of these writings was so important. We have established that we can have confidence in the claim that the Gospels are within a generation of the events they describe, and the authors had access to first-hand accounts. This is not later legendary material.

If the accounts are not legendary, then we can also add that there is no credible evidence of some kind of conspiracy or lunacy in their composition. The four accounts are different enough to demonstrate the independence of the four traditions. There is certainly some kind of shared material among them, but the divergence shows that they are presenting this quite differently. Furthermore, the differences of detail and chronology, sometimes an embarrassment to apologists, actually bolster their credibility. We may not be sure in what order events took place, but we are only encouraged in our confidence that the events *did* take place, given that we have independent records of them. The Gospels also demonstrate clarity of thought and composition. They are not wild reports that might imply deluded authorship. Anyone reading them can recognize how sane, thoughtful and considered the final composition is.

Following David Hume's scepticism, many critics would argue that it is more likely that the apostles were deceived than that a miracle took place. This argument is based on a naturalistic assumption that miracles don't happen. Therefore, no matter how unlikely, a lie is a preferable explanation to a miracle. It is worth asking our critic what historical evidence would be necessary to demonstrate that the resurrection had taken place. For some, there would never be enough evidence because miracles simply don't happen – for such sceptics, their worldview becomes a blinker. There are two facts that everyone has to explain. The first is the existence of the church itself. Where did it come from? What motivated its early origins and successful spread? A romanticized, airbrushed view of early church history might suggest that the disciples spread a deluded message because they were happy doing so, or even that they benefited materially from spreading mere rumour. The reality is that early Christians lived lives of honesty and integrity. They were willing to die for their faith in the risen Jesus in the midst of a Roman Empire rotten to the core with cruelty, injustice and compromise. Would they really have lived lives of such integrity without any hope of material gain, and in many cases only to receive persecution, oppression and even execution, if it were all built on a lie? What got Christianity started, when for its first 200 or so years it was a minority religion that brought its followers great stress and suffering? A genuine faith and confidence in the resurrection of Jesus is certainly the most plausible answer.

The second fact everyone needs to explain is the empty tomb. There is no sensible doubt that Jesus was a man who actually lived and died. However, without the resurrection it is very difficult to explain his missing body. Why did no tradition of the veneration of the resting place of the body of Jesus develop? If the authorities wanted to suppress

Christianity, why didn't they simply produce the body? Given that the disciples were preaching in the very city where Jesus had been buried, surely their message would have been ludicrous with the decaying body of Jesus lying within a mile of their words?

Some recent critical scholarship has denied that Jesus was ever buried. A number of theologians argue that the body of Jesus would have been discarded, along with the remains of other crucified victims, with the rubbish of Jerusalem. John Dominic Crossan suggests that the body of Jesus was discarded and eaten by wild animals. John Hick imagines that the body may have been burned with the garbage and reduced to lime.

But these attempts to dismiss the Gospel records are unconvincing. The record of the burial of Jesus is common to the four Gospel accounts and extra-biblical writings. The fact that Jesus is buried in a borrowed and not a family tomb would have been an embarrassing admission to a first-century Jewish writer for whom these things were important. Furthermore, we have archaeological evidence that crucified victims were buried. In the Israel Museum you can see the ankle and wrist bones of a crucified victim from the first century. Corroded nails attached to wooden remains are still visible. Placed in an ossuary and identified as Yohan Ben Ha'galgol, this body had been given the same burial as any other first-century Jew.

The traditional reasons for rejecting the resurrection of Jesus include suggestions that the apostles were frauds (they stole the body) or deceived (they were hallucinating). These objections take a dim view of the disciples' character. It certainly seems implausible to suggest that first-century revolutionaries who would teach selfless love and honesty for no personal gain, and sometimes only to receive pain, would do so on the basis of a deceptive conspiracy. As for hallucination, the proponent has to explain a miracle witnessed by large numbers of people at one time and subjected to years of careful, reflective thought. Did they really not spot the flaw in their own tradition? After all, this suggestion also has to explain the fact that the body was still resting in Jerusalem. Loyal followers would have developed pilgrimages to the resting place. Hostile critics would have pointed to its location as a persuasive counter-argument. That such a historically testable claim should have been at the centre of a faith makes it hard to see how it could have got off the ground if the claim had not been true. It is also important to stress that the Christian claim that Jesus had risen from the dead was not some common tale told about dead leaders. The early Christians were Jewish, and Judaism taught the resurrection, not resuscitation, of the body as its transformation for eternal life.

> We know of lots of other messianic and similar movements in the Jewish world roughly contemporary with Jesus. In many cases the leader died a violent death at the hands of the authorities. In not one single case do we hear the slightest mention of the disappointed followers claiming that their hero had been raised from the dead. They knew better. 'Resurrection' was not a private event. It involved human bodies. There would have to be an empty tomb somewhere.[13]

In what sense unique?

The uniqueness of Jesus is not a claim about a particular miracle or event associated with him. After all, by that standard everyone is unique. Jesus is unique in the New Testament claim that he is 'God with us' (Matthew 1:23). Other prophets and teachers have been thought of as good models of divinity,

194 | CHRISTIAN CONFIDENCE

and they themselves have presented a message from the Divine. Jesus is unique in claiming that he is the one and only Son of God. This makes him different from all other people and, of particular relevance, different from the leaders of any other major religious tradition.

Is the claim that Jesus died and rose from the dead simply one instance of a common dying-and-rising Redeemer-God myth from the ancient world? This claim is often made. Parallels are drawn between the story of Jesus and myths concerning Osiris, a dying and rising deity from Egypt, and the cult of Mithra. The myth of a god who is defeated and dies, only to be reborn and rise, fitted well with the cycle of the seasons and the progression from the dead of winter to the rebirth of spring.

In the 2008 film *Religulous*, Bill Maher presents a contemptuous attack on Christianity in which he claims fourteen parallels between the myth of Horus and the Gospel accounts of Jesus. These include a virgin birth, being baptized by a baptizer who was then himself beheaded, walking on water, miraculously raising El-Azarus (Lazarus?) from the dead, and being crucified. The parallels sound stunning. Until we realize that they are not true. The entire sequence in the *Religulous* film is fabrication. Horus, being a child of gods, has an odd conception involving Isis and her murdered husband's remains, but it is not a virgin birth in historic time and space. There is no reference to Horus being baptized, walking on water (as a sky god who could fly, why on earth would he need to?), no reference to anyone called El-Azarus or to being crucified.

So if these alleged parallels are all pure fiction, then what makes them appear so credible to a contemporary film-maker? There are superficial resemblances. In Egyptian iconography, there is a popular image of Isis suckling her baby Horus that echoes the imagery of Mary and the infant Jesus. In many mythological stories, gods and heroes return from death, but these are not to be confused with stories of real human beings returning to life. Interestingly, the resurrection stories of pagan gods (Dionysius, Adonis) are all later in date than the New Testament.[14] Craig Blomberg surveys a range of parallels and concludes with the often-cited cult of Mithra:

> Mithraism began to resemble Christianity only in the late second and early third centuries. But all of these developments are too late to have influenced the first Christian writers; if anything, they may have been born out of a desire to make their heroes look more like Jesus and therefore more credible in a world in which Christianity was coming to have greater influence.[15]

Therefore, even the superficial resemblances do not provide evidence for a long pre-Christ tradition. But what does this parallel really tell us anyway? The longer and louder an assertion is made (preferably within a slick film production), the more credible bogus claims appear to be.

Apologists have always had to deal with the claim that the New Testament does not teach the divinity of Christ. Among the early church thinkers, this was a recurrent debate. The direct references to Jesus being God are numerous (John 1:1; Romans 9:5; Colossians 2:9; Hebrews 1:3); however, there are many subtleties in the text. In fact, it can be fairly said that the New Testament does not state, 'Jesus is God' in such simple terms. Instead, it identifies the things that Jesus said and did with the things that only God can do (Mark 2:1–11). It places the name of Jesus in the rank of the name of God (for example, compare Philippians 2:6–11 with Isaiah 45:22–24). This explains how Jesus revealed his own identity in the Gospel accounts. He did not give an extended explanation of the doctrine of the Trinity, nor simply state, 'I am God.' Instead, Jesus did all those things that only God can do and allowed people to draw their own conclusions. On one occasion, four friends brought a paralysed man to Jesus, hoping that he would be healed. The first reaction of Jesus was to declare, 'Son, your sins are forgiven.' The response of the religious leaders was appropriate: 'He's blaspheming! Who can forgive sins but God alone?' (Mark 2:7). They knew their Scriptures and understood the implications of what Jesus was claiming to be able to do.

This is the background to a famous argument put forward by C. S. Lewis called the 'trilemma'. It is a trilemma because it forces us to choose one of three interpretations of the identity of Jesus. Given his claims to divinity, Jesus is either a madman, a wicked man or exactly who he claimed to be: the Son of God. Lewis himself borrowed the argument from G. K. Chesterton in *The Everlasting Man* (1925), which he described as the most influential book on his own life. Chesterton deals with the popular idea that Jesus was origin-ally a good moral teacher, distorted into something else by later church tradition. He turns the argument on its head by pointing out that in the Gospels we meet a man who can be disturbing and does not fit our neat categories; only later in church tradition is he softened and domesticated into something easier on the mind's eye. The Jesus of the Gospels is mad, bad, or who he claimed to be: God with us.

This is a significant argument, though it is received with scorn in some quarters. For example, Richard Dawkins lightly dismisses it: 'Even if that evidence were good, the trilemma on offer would be ludicrously inadequate. A fourth pos-sibility, almost too obvious to need mentioning, is that Jesus was honestly mistaken. Plenty of people are.'[16] This seems plausible. Jesus might have been honestly mistaken that he had supernatural powers. Plenty of people are. He might have been honestly mistaken that God had spoken to him. Plenty of people are. But we have to take into account the magnitude of the claim Jesus was making for himself. In the first-century Jewish context, there was an absolute commitment to monotheism. Visible representations of the divine were blasphemous. A first-century Jew claiming to be one with the Father, or to forgive sins, or to command the elements, was to claim a divine status that deserved the death penalty in that culture. This was not an 'honestly mistaken' individual. This was either madness or wickedness.

In a similar vein to Dawkins, Christopher Hitchens rails against Lewis's reasoning as 'so pathetic as to defy description' and as 'a crude non sequitur'.[17] His charge is, like Dawkins, that there is a fourth option. The option he prefers is that the Gospels are not literal history. They are layers of hearsay, written upon hearsay far removed from historical facts. Hitchens is heavily reliant on the popular work of Bart Ehrman. Ehrman is a formidable New Testament scholar and critic of evangelical Christianity. Having trained at Moody Bible Institute, an American evangelical college, he understands the conservative view of the Bible to which he is now opposed. Ehrman's engagement with the Bible emphasizes the problems in the text and argues that early Christianity was diverse and contradictory in its beliefs and ideas. There is nothing new in the details Ehrman points out – scholars of all persuasion have wrestled with the possible problems and resolutions of these details for centuries. Ehrman's work simply reminds us that establishing the reliability of the text will be a never-ending scholarly debate, but the far more important point is to establish the historicity of Jesus, his death and his resurrection. When we do this, we close Hitchens' preferred option, that the Gospels are a collection of hearsay and rumour.

A unique salvation

A significant proportion of the Gospels is taken up with a description and explanation of the death of Jesus. The reason for this is that the message of the cross would become the focus of the good news message that Christians would preach and share. When Jesus died on the cross, he bore a penalty for the wrongdoing of all human history. Christianity is unique in emphasizing that our deeds, sacrifices and ceremonies cannot add anything to the finished work of Christ. It is by grace we are saved – this is a gift of God (Ephesians 2:8).

An obvious objection to the uniqueness of the gospel is to ask about the fate of the unevangelized. What about those who have never heard? In many ways this is a very pressing concern, both for apologetics and as a pastoral issue for those who come to faith from other religions.

As a question for apologetics, it is closely related to the issue of why God allows pain and suffering. Why does a good God allow a universe in which not everyone is saved? It is important to clarify that the Bible teaches God's universal love and desire that all people be saved (Ezekiel 18:23; 1 Timothy 2:3–4). Whether all people will be saved or not depends on our response to the gospel (Acts 17:30: 'God . . . commands all people everywhere to repent'). The reason that some are lost is not because God is hard on us, but because we are hardened to God. We prefer not to admit our fault and cast ourselves on God's love and mercy. It is true that God could have created a universe without people who are lost, but it is not clear that we can understand what such a universe would be like. It would not be a universe in which there were people like us, with the capacity to rebel and reject the love of God. Whatever else it would be, it would not be this universe.

In the context of world religions, those who raise the issue of salvation generally wonder whether salvation is possible through non-Christian religions or before Christ came into the world or among those dying in infancy. It is no bad thing for us to admit that this is one of many areas where we have no definitive answer. We are not God, and we must trust in his judgments and not in our own. However, the Bible leads us to have some glimmer of an answer.

It is tempting to suggest that those who die beyond the reach of the gospel are not culpable. This is certainly a plausible answer in regard to those dying in infancy – though we remember the words of David:

> Surely I was sinful at birth,
>   sinful from the time my mother conceived me.
> (Psalm 51:5)

All people are under God's judgment and deserve condemnation. Our default position as human beings is to be separated from God. This is the basic problem of the human condition, to which the gospel is an answer.

There is no salvation outside of Christ and his atoning work in taking the judgment of God upon himself on the cross. We do know that this atoning work applied to all people of faith prior to the time of Jesus. They had trusted in Christ without knowing his name. This is true of the Old Testament saints. Of course, in many cases they benefited from indirect knowledge of Christ through the Old Testament revelation. But not always. Some of the people of faith in the Bible were outside of the Old Testament covenant, but still had a real knowledge of God (Jethro, Job and Melchizedek are all intriguing examples).

So it seems reasonable to admit that it is possible that God is able to bring to himself anyone who would have genuine faith in him. How this might happen is not revealed in Scripture. Norman Anderson, a scholar of law and Islam, probably gave as full an answer as Scripture would permit to explain such a possibility:

> I believe there is much, in the Bible and experience, to point to the fact that God *can*, and sometimes does, work directly in men's hearts to convict them of sin and prompt them to throw themselves on his mercy.[18]

This response acknowledges a possibility without undermining the necessity of the death of Christ and our need for personal faith. If someone outside the reach of the gospel comes to a saving knowledge of God, then that must be in spite of their religious culture, not through it. Whether this is possible without direct revelation is beyond our knowledge, and we must simply trust in the justice and wisdom of God (Genesis 18:25). It does not help our case for Christianity to pronounce boldly on things we do not know, or to promote wishful speculations as certainties. This leads us to perhaps the most difficult question of all.

10. Everybody hurts

Take away the cross of Christ, and the Bible is a dark book.
J. C. Ryle

The great question

It is hard to imagine a question that comes up with more regularity than that of suffering and evil. Why does God permit bad things to happen? This question has troubled all sorts of people throughout history. Because of its universal significance, it is an important area for Christian witness and debate.

However, it is interesting to note Alister McGrath's observation that 'Christian writers prior to the seventeenth century did not believe that suffering posed any serious threat to Christian belief.'[1] Of course, it has always been a pastoral problem for faith. The book of Job, Luke 13:1–5, James 1:2–4, along with many other examples, demonstrate that this has been a persistent theme of biblical reflection.

But only since the Enlightenment has the problem of evil been seen as such a strong reason against God. It is ironic that, while throughout most of history when people have suffered greatly they have found good reasons for faith, in an age of relative security, longevity and improving health-care this has become a reason not to believe. Perhaps it reflects an overly intellectual approach to the problem: in the past it was not so much a question of why God allows suffering, but how we should deal with the suffering that inevitably comes our way.

Everyone suffers to some extent. When someone is going through a painful experience, loss or anxiety, they probably need comfort and a listening ear rather than a defence of the Christian faith. But the experience does generate criticisms of the credibility of Christianity, to which we need to give an answer.

So what do we mean by suffering? Under this heading, many diverse experiences or events may be implied. There are natural disasters such as earthquakes and tornados. The problem here is complicated by the fact that there is presumably nothing intrinsically evil about the plate tectonics that cause earthquakes or the air currents that create tornados. These are natural phenomena, to be expected on a rocky terrestrial planet with an atmosphere like ours. What makes them relevant here is when they cause suffering and misery to people through their timing, location and intensity. Also under this heading, we might mean pain, illness and disease. But what is pain? We know that pain is a good thing, necessary for our body to function properly. Pain is a warning alarm in our nervous system to alert us to dangers. Those who suffer from conditions that prevent them from feeling pain are in a far worse state than those who actually feel pain. Therefore, it is the causes of the pain, its intensity and our inability to resolve those causes that is the real issue.

A distinct area of the problem of evil is the suffering caused by other people: murder, rape and violence, not to mention gossip and cheating. Our physical capabilities can be twisted to do evil deeds.

So the problem of suffering is really a problem of misery. It is the sadness and misery of creatures (human or not) that we identify as the real issue. So why does God allow people to experience misery? C. S. Lewis described the problem with precision:

> If God were good, he would wish to make his creatures perfectly happy, and if God were almighty he would be able to do what he wished. But the creatures are not happy. Therefore, God lacks either the goodness, or power, or both. That is the problem of pain in its simplest form.[2]

Stating the problem logically helps to identify what we are really asking. The objection concerns a perceived contradiction in these three statements:

(a) God is perfectly powerful
(b) God is completely good
(c) There is suffering and evil in the world

The reason why this counts against the existence of God is explained by the following conclusion:

(d) A good and powerful God would eliminate all suffering. Therefore, the good and powerful God does not exist.

It does not follow from this that no god could exist. But the God who exists in a universe of suffering must either be less powerful than we had thought, or less good than we had thought. Some apologists have been led down this path.

Perhaps God is unable to control the future. Perhaps God is limited in his power or knowledge so that he is unable to control events, but can only respond to them with the limited resources and knowledge available to him. This way of answering the question has been promoted recently by a movement called Open Theism. Gregory Boyd argues that this is a necessary limitation for God because he has chosen to create a world in which there are genuine, freely chosen relationships:

> If God created a world where love is possible, he thereby ruled out a world in which his will is always done. If he chooses to create this kind of world, he can't guarantee that his will is always done, not because he lacks the power but *because of the kind of world he created.*[3]

This answer has its attractions as an apologetic strategy because it seems to absolve God of any guilt or responsibility.

But there is a price to pay. Many other implications need to be addressed. An important implication for the Open Theists is that it also follows that God does not know the future. If God already knew the future, then our decisions and actions would not be genuinely free. Therefore, God is also limited in his knowledge of the future. But if this is the case, then God is learning as time goes by. God is not the all-powerful, sovereign Being governing all of creation. He is one agent among many, seeking the best, but preferring a hands-off approach to his creation. The implications lead to a revision of the doctrine of God, which for many Christians is a price too high to pay.

However, the general point Boyd makes may still be very valuable in apologetics. It is true that the 'will' of God is a word with some ambiguity. To be honest is the will of God. To murder is not the will of God. In this sense, 'will' expresses what God desires of us. But there is a deeper sense of the will of God which means his sovereign or almighty power. Nothing can happen which he does not permit, allow or ordain. Some Christians prefer to speak of God 'permitting' evil rather than 'ordaining' evil, but they generally agree that God works all things together for his ultimate good and perfect will.

There is another way of addressing this question that does not require redefining God's power or sovereignty. This is to provide a reason *why* God might permit suffering. If there is a morally sufficient reason for the perfectly powerful and completely good God to allow suffering, then this is no reason to doubt his existence. Indeed, to describe God as 'all-powerful' does not imply that God can do anything. The Bible itself says that God cannot lie or repent as a person does. We might add that God cannot create a square circle or a married bachelor. These are not constraints upon God, simply a reflection of the nature of God who is a God of love, goodness, order and meaning. So perhaps there is a reason why a God of power chooses to create a universe like the one in which we live? As we survey various possible answers to the problem of suffering, we will see that Christians have been trying to discern and provide this reason. While it may be possible to supply a general answer, we are unlikely to have reasons for specific forms of suffering. Trusting that God has his reasons is not the same as knowing what those reasons may be. In dealing with the subject, C. S. Lewis challenges what we mean by God being 'good'. Too often this becomes a trivial description, implying that God never means harm. But what if there were a valid reason for harm – whether to bring judgment or reformation? Harm is not always harmful. God's primary concern in human history may not be to keep people safe and happy. Perhaps his purposes are greater and more testing than that?

The various answers that apologists have offered over the years are called 'theodicies', which means attempts to defend the justice of God. One very ancient attempt at an answer is called the 'greater-good' theodicy. The early church theologian Irenaeus (c. AD 130–202) is associated with this treatment of the problem of evil, particularly because of the more recent work of John Hick. According to Hick, Irenaeus emphasized the nature of the world and human history as an environment ideal for helping us to become better people. It is true that it is not the best environment for keeping people safe or happy or comfortable. If God had intended that, then perhaps he would have created a different universe. But our environment is ideal for helping us become the people God wants us to be. Creation has two stages: in the beginning people were 'intelligent animals endowed with the capacity for immense moral and spiritual development', but in our present era they 'are gradually being transformed through their own free responses'[4] into something better:

> This world with all its 'heartaches and the thousand natural shocks that flesh is heir to', an environment so manifestly not designed for the maximisation of human pleasure and the minimisation of human pain, may nevertheless be rather well adapted to the quite different purpose of 'soul-making'.[5]

This is sometimes called the 'greater-good defence' because it claims that the existence of evil leads to a greater good than would have been possible without it. The implication of the argument is that the fall of Adam and Eve was in some sense a necessary step in our growth towards goodness. We are better off for it. But Francis Schaeffer disputed Hick's ideas in the light of the Christian doctrine of creation. According to Schaeffer, the problem with this theodicy is that it takes things the way they are (a world of suffering) and assumes that is how they have always been, and that God intended it to be that way. Schaeffer stressed the historic significance of the fall of Adam and Eve in space and time. Regardless of the issues of when and how exactly these events took place, creation now is not the same as it was before the fall:

> Non-Christian philosophers almost universally agree in seeing everything as normal, assuming things are as they have always been. The Christian sees things now as not the way they have always been. And, of course, this is very important to the explanation of evil in the world.[6]

Many attempts to explain evil start and finish with the way things are. The biblical account of history follows a different course. God created a beautiful paradise – in need of shaping and populating, but without sin and evil. Through rebellion, on earth and in heaven, our environment has changed and become subject to death and decay (Romans 8:20–21). Even if, with an old-earth creation model, we accept that death and decay were part of the animal kingdom prior to the fall, we still assume that the special conditions of the garden in Eden were without misery for Adam and Eve.

However, the greater-good defence is stronger when it takes into account the future purposes of God. After all, there is a sense in which the new creation of biblical prophecy is far better than the old creation of Genesis. For one thing, men and women will know what it means to have been redeemed and forgiven – something which Adam and Eve could not have understood prior to the fall. John Milton, in his epic poem *Paradise Lost*, has Adam stand on a high hill and see a prophetic vision of the whole of history spread out before him, including the coming of Christ and the new creation. He cries out,

O goodness infinite, goodness immense!
That all this good of evil shall produce,
And evil turn to good; more wonderful
Than that which by creation first brought forth
Light out of darkness! Full of doubt I stand,
Whether I should repent me now of sin
By me done and occasioned, or rejoice
Much more, that much more good thereof shall spring,
To God more glory, more good will to men
From God, and over wrath grace shall abound.[7]

For all the attractions of this interpretation of evil, there are many reasons to be careful in using it. For example, it risks turning evil into a good. Evil becomes a necessary instrument God must use in order to make immature creatures holy. Rather than being a punishment upon sin (judgment) or a rebellion against God (both human and demonic), evil becomes the necessary process God uses to shape human beings. Evil is not so bad after all! Nonetheless, this approach may cast some light on why God has chosen to create a universe in which there could be a fall and consequent misery for the human race.

The most influential theodicy of recent times is probably Alvin Plantinga's 'free-will defence'.[8] This states that evil originates with the choices of free people who do bad things. God is not responsible for evil, only for creating the conditions in which evil was possible. Could God have created a universe without evil? Yes, but to do so he would have created a universe without free will, and therefore not this universe we are part of. To ask for a universe like ours without evil would be like asking God to create a square circle. As we have already noted, there are some things God cannot do.

As a response to the problem of evil, there is great strength in the free-will defence. It puts the emphasis on human responsibility rather than on divine decree. But there are problems. First, it is still difficult to establish the link between natural disasters and free will. We all know that someone is responsible when there is murder or theft. But who is responsible for tornados, floods and earthquakes? Secondly, Christians are committed to the idea that men and women can be truly free only in perfect obedience. Jesus Christ was truly free in perfect obedience. God is perfectly free in always acting with pure love and wisdom. As Christians, we find our freedom in obedience as slaves to Christ. In the new creation there will be no more sin and pain, so our freedom will be perfected, and we will freely choose never to rebel or sin again.

Many evangelicals would wish to avoid giving any answer that fails to reflect the biblical balance between human responsibility and divine sovereignty. To affirm that God wills all things can be dangerously fatalistic and undermine the biblical teaching that we are responsible for our sin and its consequences. To deny that God is in control, even over evil acts, can be attractive but undermines the biblical teaching that God is sovereign over all things and works all things together for a greater plan. God is not taken by surprise, and his goal is always achieved, even though the route may be circuitous. An answer that holds these biblical themes together is called 'compatibilism'. This approach provides helpful boundaries for any Christian answer that seeks to remain within the parameters of biblical teaching.

Compatibilism recognizes that the Bible teaches two themes that could be seen as contradictory. First, God is in control of all history, knowing the beginning from the end, and working all things for his own purpose. Secondly, created beings have responsibility for their own actions which they freely choose, and for which they must face the consequences.

The biblical writers are unembarrassed at this apparent contradiction. Consider the words of Joseph in the Old Testament, when referring to his brothers selling him into slavery, an action that would in time bring him to a position of power in Egypt: 'You intended to harm me, but God intended it for good to accomplish what is now being done, the saving of many lives' (Genesis 50:20). People are responsible for what they choose to do. This is not because God has taken his hands off the steering wheel and let us have a go. It is because we are responsible for our actions and choices, regardless of whether or not we could have chosen otherwise. Perhaps we felt constrained or compelled to do wrong? We are still responsible. Some explanation along these lines makes sense of how Judas Iscariot can be personally responsible, even though his actions fulfil biblical prophecy (John 13:26–30). Paul Helm calls this a 'no-risk' view of providence.[9] This certainly safeguards a strong view of the sovereignty of God, though critics argue that it contradicts the common-sense meaning of 'free will'.

All of these Christian answers point to some kind of greater-good explanation. They all assume that God could have created a universe without evil if he had wished to, but that there is some reason why he created the universe that he did. We do not have simple, soundbite answers, but we do have the reflections of the people of Scripture who were familiar with suffering and had grounds to trust God regardless (Genesis 18:25; Job 1:20–22; Hebrews 11:39). We also have the remarkable evidence of Christian history and experience: the church has grown through suffering and persecution, and believers have often matured through their own struggles and setbacks. Often testimony of our own personal response to suffering and evil can carry great weight in addressing this question.

Alternative explanations

Though the Bible does not provide a neat resolution or sound-bite answer to the problem of evil, it does shed important light on the issue, and many people will find this at least helps them to deal with its existence.

But a more compelling strategy may be to reverse the question and ask about the alternative to the biblical world-view. There are in fact many alternatives, and all of them share troubling features.

A very ancient alternative to Christianity is called 'dualism'. Augustine wrote against this view, as it was found among a religious group called the Manichaeans. Dualism teaches that good and evil are equal and opposite forces in the universe. These two powers are in conflict with each other. Augustine knew that the Bible taught that only God is all-powerful – there can be no equal but opposing force to him. But Augustine also found help in the philosophy of Aristotle in order to develop his apologetic against dualism. Aristotle had noted that negative things are actually an absence of something good to which they correspond: darkness is an absence of light, weakness an absence of strength. So evil should not be understood as an independent power, but only as a lack of what is good. Therefore, evil is a failure to choose what is morally good or right. This evil may occur among people or in a supernatural realm (fallen angels), but it impacts in some way on the natural order itself.

So the origins of evil are not a power that exists apart from God, or even a power that God wanted to create. Evil is a corruption or distortion of the good that God has made. The biblical view is that the world as we know it is not as God intended it to be. It has been corrupted, tainted and damaged by sin, natural and supernatural. Evil is neither an independent power nor a part of God's nature.

If the Manichaeans were in danger of elevating evil too highly, the most popular alternative today is in danger of dismissing it altogether. For all their virulent opposition to Christianity, the new-atheist writers have no absolute basis for identifying anything as evil.

Atheism, as we have seen, endorses a materialist view of the universe. There is no God or universal moral law by which we may judge right and wrong. Where then does our moral sense come from? Richard Dawkins is entirely logical to take his materialistic worldview to its conclusions and state that altruism (selfless care for others) is actually a selfish impulse arising from our instinctive need to preserve and multiply our genes. How else will a society be stable enough to provide a successful context for raising children? Therefore 'Natural selection favours genes that predispose individuals, in relationships of asymmetric need and opportunity, to give when they can, and to solicit giving when they can't.'[10] Evolution does not simply favour animals that can live with others and reproduce successfully; it also favours those who have an urge to be kind or generous. Therefore, we end up with a human race which is far kinder than it needs to be for mere survival. But Dawkins is clear: this is a mistake, or by-product, of evolution:

> We can no more help ourselves feeling pity when we see a weeping unfortunate (who is unrelated and unable to reciprocate) than we can help ourselves feeling lust for a member of the opposite sex (who may be infertile or otherwise unable to reproduce). Both are misfirings, Darwinian mistakes: blessed, precious mistakes.[11]

If natural selection worked consistently, the world would be a cold and heartless place, so thank nature it does not! But herein lies the problem: where is the standard by which we describe these mistakes as 'blessed' and 'precious'? The moral standard is no longer simply a description of the material universe, but something transcendent. Perhaps Dawkins means 'blessed to me' or 'I like it'. But that is not a moral standard, just a statement of personal taste. The woman raped in Rwanda by the cruel soldier finds nothing 'blessed' in the act. So how do we discern between evil misfirings and blessed ones? Dawkins compares sexual lust with the lust to be compassionate, and describes both as the misfiring of natural selection. But we recoil from the obvious consequence and need to draw upon the transcendent categories of good and evil in order to distinguish between the misfirings that are a blessing and those that are not. Materialism lacks the explanatory power to make sense of such distinctions. Christianity, by contrast, offers explanatory power, giving definitions to good and evil which are not simply descriptive of natural processes. It gives a reason to take sides.

The only basis for morality, according to a materialist view, is functional. That is to say, the good is whatever helps produce beneficial results. Therefore, good behaviour is that which helps us live alongside one another and provide a peaceable society in which to go about our lives: 'Don't do to others what you would not want them doing to you' goes the simple golden rule (or, more accurately, the silver rule). But this is no basis for morality. It is a basis for identifying some forms of behaviour as better suited to producing a peaceful society, but it assumes that a peaceful society is a good thing. Why should I share in that project? What if I choose to behave differently? The materialist is trying to squeeze an 'ought' statement out of an 'is' statement. The statement: 'This behaviour leads to a peaceful society' provides no grounds for the statement: 'You ought to want a peaceful society.' C. S. Lewis identifies this flaw: 'From propositions about fact alone no *practical* conclusion can ever be drawn. *This will preserve society* cannot lead to *do this* except by the mediation of *society ought to be preserved.*'[12]

This leads to the moral argument for God which is a very powerful apologetic. The failure of the materialist alternative is that it has no basis for defining how we ought to behave. Moral values can be nothing more than subjective choices. But, in practice, few people admit this. This is because most people have some sense in which moral values are like facts or laws. It is wrong to murder, and we tend to believe this regardless of our opinion on the existence of God. Of course, there may be circumstances where something that looked like murder really is not – perhaps killing someone in war or in self-defence. That is why we have ethical debates and moral reasoning. But the disputed areas still prove the point. We have transcendent values of goodness that apply at all times and in all places. Few people will justify the anti-Semitism of Nazi Germany, the slave trade of the eighteenth century or any examples of child abuse or rape. Such behaviour is wrong. The moral argument takes this intuition as a starting point in building the case for God. Atheists and theists can agree that objective moral values exist. Atheists can be good, moral people. The argument is not that you have to be a Christian in order to be moral.

But if we do believe that there are objective moral values or laws, then who made these laws or where did they come from? Perhaps they just 'are', in the same way natural laws like gravity or magnetism simply 'are'. However, moral laws are not the same as natural laws. They are not simply descriptions of natural processes. Moral laws are to do with will, purpose and intention. Therefore, they are better explained by a personal moral Law-giver who himself has a will, a purpose and an intention. The existence of objective moral values is good grounds for assuming the existence of a divine, moral Law-giver.

Christianity as a force for good

Christianity provides a satisfying basis for belief in objective moral values. It provides us with a definition of good and evil. It gives reasons for why evil exists, even if no single reason satisfies every problem. While there are intellectual puzzles to be solved, Christians down through the centuries have been motivated by their faith to counter evil.

The aggressive new atheists have attempted to undermine this claim by suggesting that religion is the root of all evil. It is true that in the name of religion evil has been done – perhaps sometimes even by those who were sincerely misguided. But the same is also true of atheism. In the name of atheism (the regimes of Stalin and Pol Pot come to mind, along with the quasi-occult, anti-Christian diatribes of Adolf Hitler), evil has been done. That beliefs can be misused for evil ends does not in itself undermine the beliefs themselves.

In fact, we might go further and point out that atheism provides a better justification for evil behaviour than Christianity. After all, if there is no God to whom we must give an account, and if we cannot be sure that our moral beliefs are universally valid, then why should we keep to them? And if we find that a practice which seems evil could help in the preservation or purification of our society, then why not do it? Thank God that atheists are not always consistent with their convictions! But what if they are? The implications for ethics in a world without a transcendent moral law should strike fear into the heart of the staunchest supporter of Richard Dawkins.

But is religion really the root of evil? We can respond to this by pointing out the great good that religious people have done over the centuries. Faith in their God has caused Christians to take a high view of human life and dignity.

In classical Greek and Roman society, it was not unusual to allow unwanted children to die. Christians opposed this mistreatment of the vulnerable. Tertullian (c. AD 160–240), an apologist whom we have already noted, argued against killing or abandoning children. It was a concern of many early Christians and led to the abolition of infanticide by Emperor Valentinian in AD 374. The 'orphanage' was an idea of early church leaders, Basil of Caesarea and Chrysostom of Constantinople. This practical initiative has been continued down through the centuries by Christians of all persuasions. George Müller (1805–98) founded orphanages in Bristol, England that would provide care for over 10,000 children. The abuse of Native American peoples by Western settlers was opposed by significant Christian leaders such as Bartolomé de Las Casas (1484–1566), William Penn (1644–1718) and Jonathan Edwards (1703–58). One of the greatest figures in the abolition of the slave trade was the Christian parliamentarian William Wilberforce (1759–1833). In the area of racial prejudice, one immediately thinks of Martin Luther King (1929–68), or in the case of the poor in India, Mother Teresa (1910–97). The abolition of the Hindu practice of burning widows alive on the funeral pyres of their dead husbands was achieved primarily by the efforts of the Baptist missionary, William Carey (1761–1834). These people were motivated by their faith in God and the teachings of Jesus. Indeed, the silver rule to which we referred earlier was not actually what Jesus taught. The moral instinct not to do to others what you would not have done to yourself is a pretty poor moral standard indeed. It simply means avoiding causing harm. Jesus expressed a far higher standard: 'Do to others as you would have them do to you' (Luke 6:31). This is a stronger, more positive command actively to want to do for others what you would want done for yourself. Unlike the silver rule, which simply prohibits nasty behaviour, the golden rule inspires social reform and active participation in bringing health and healing to all of society. This was the motivation for Wilberforce, Luther King, Mother Teresa. In the name of Christianity, people have done wicked things, but in the light of Christ's teaching, people have been a force for great good.

The conquering Christ

The problem of suffering is a repeated theme throughout the Bible. That is one reason why it should not take us by surprise. While we may not have easy answers and may experience trauma in this life, the biblical story persuades us that this world is not the way God intended it to be.

The world was corrupted and changed through the rebellion of Adam and Eve (Genesis 3:13–19). Our own sinful behaviour and distorted use of free will contribute to the ongoing effects of this rebellion (Romans 1:28–32).

For all this suffering and sin, God has provided a remedy. The Father God sent his own Son, Jesus, into this fallen world to take upon himself the punishment sin deserves. Jesus, a man of perfect goodness, obedience and love, suffered the criminal's death of crucifixion under Roman law. The Father God allowed his own Son to suffer the consequences of our human rebellion.

In his life, Jesus knew rejection and spite. In his death, he knew pain and separation. His suffering was both the physical suffering of human agony and also a spiritual suffering we can barely understand. Jesus suffered the righteous anger of his own Father against all the godlessness and evil of human history. Whatever wickedness people have done, Jesus suffered a punishment fit for the crime. That is the Christian explanation of the cross. He who knew no sin became sin for us (2 Corinthians 5:21).

When Jesus rose from the dead, his resurrection was not simply to provide a piece of miraculous evidence for our apologetics. He had conquered the consequences of sin, suffering and death. Through the cross, we could now know forgiveness and a foretaste of the new creation. The resurrection body of Jesus could become our body too if we joined him in faith.

The new creation is the real resolution of human history. Justice against sin will be executed. But forgiveness and mercy will reign. All those who trust in Jesus Christ as their dying Saviour and risen Lord will be transformed into people of a new age where he will wipe every tear from their eyes. There will be 'no more death or mourning or crying or pain' (Revelation 21:4).

This is no fairy tale. The trustworthiness of the Bible provides a sure account of where we have come from, what has gone wrong and what God will one day do about it.

Christian apologetics is nothing more than a conversation leading to the cross. After roadblocks are removed and alternatives denied, we reach the solution to the problem of sin and evil. Any apologetic that does not ultimately lead to Christ crucified is not properly an example of Christian apologetics.

In the cross we know that God has entered the world of suffering and pain. On the cross Jesus identifies with us in our sadness and hurt. Through the cross Jesus has conquered all evil and rebellion. Now the answer to the problem of suffering is not to be found simply in an intellectual explanation, but in personal faith in the saving work of Christ.

We can have confidence in our conversations because we have confidence in the conquering Christ.

Conclusion

This has been a wide-ranging journey! We have explored Christian thought over the centuries and different objections raised against the faith. I hope you have identified principles that you have been able to apply in your own life. We need to reflect on how to present the case for our faith both clearly and warmly. Christians down through the ages have done so too.

One lesson that I think becomes clear in this kind of survey is that Christians have ample reason to be confident, even if we do not know all the answers. If we are not sure of an answer or can see problems in the answers that some Christians give, then we are not the first to do so. Christians have disagreed among themselves over the method of apologetics, the specific issues of evolutionary theory and why God permits suffering. But none of this need detract from the confidence of our witness. Sometimes sharing the fact that Christians themselves dispute certain questions is part of our witness. It does not show weakness but strength. We care about the truth and so we will debate among ourselves the proper interpretation of Genesis. We are gospel people, with generous hearts and sincere minds. Christianity can be robust in its commitment to the infallibility of the Bible, while gracious in its disputes over how that Word is understood.

This lesson then informs our witness to the world. We should confront false ideologies and misleading objections whenever we can. But we do so with grace and love, knowing that winning an argument is not always the same thing as winning hearts and minds.

I hope this book has encouraged you to present a confident case for Christianity in your conversations, even though you may feel you still have many unanswered questions.

One thing I have noticed in my years of ministry and teaching is that there are many Christians who seem to come to faith but drift away after only a few months. Often their commitment seemed to be based merely on a subjective experience or passing feelings. When problems arise or difficult questions are asked, such faith evaporates like the morning mist.

The kind of study we have engaged in will strengthen your faith. You should not be taken by surprise by suffering or perplexing questions. My real prayer in writing this book is not simply that you might share your faith confidently with others, but that you might know what you believe more firmly, and have tools to think through new questions. As you do so, you are surrounded by a great cloud of witnesses who have gone before and now urge you to run with perseverance the race marked out for you (Hebrews 12:1–3)!

Further reading

A bibliography for a book like this could amount to many pages. This is a selective guide, providing reference to just a few exemplary texts under each subject heading. To read a couple of the books listed under each heading would equip you very thoroughly in the task of apologetics.

Textbooks on apologetics

Kenneth D. Boa and Robert M. Bowman, *Faith Has Its Reasons*, 2nd edn (Milton Keynes: Paternoster, 2006).

David K. Clark, *Dialogical Apologetics* (Grand Rapids: Baker Books, 1993).

Paul Copan and William Lane Craig (eds.), *Passionate Conviction: Contemporary Discourses on Christian Apologetics* (Nashville: B. & H. Publishing Group, 2007).

Steven B. Cowan (ed.), *Five Views on Apologetics* (Leicester: IVP, 2000).

William Lane Craig, *On Guard: Defending Your Faith with Reason and Precision* (Colorado Springs: David C. Cook, 2010).

William Lane Craig, *Reasonable Faith: Christian Truth and Apologetics* (Wheaton: Crossway, 1994).

John M. Frame, *Apologetics to the Glory of God* (Phillipsburg, New Jersey: P. & R., 1994).

John H. Gerstner, R. C. Sproul and Arthur W. Lindsley, *Classical Apologetics* (Grand Rapids: Zondervan, 1984).

Douglas Groothuis, *Christian Apologetics: A Comprehensive Case for Biblical Faith* (Downers Grove: IVP, 2011).

Peter Hicks, *Evangelicals and Truth: A Creative Proposal for a Postmodern Age* (Leicester: Apollos, 1998).

Alister McGrath, *Bridge-Building: Effective Christian Apologetics* (Leicester: IVP, 1992).

Nick Pollard, *Evangelism Made Slightly Less Difficult* (Leicester: IVP, 1997).

James W. Sire, *Why Good Arguments Often Fail: Making a More Persuasive Case for Christ* (Nottingham: IVP, 2006).

C. S. Lewis and Francis Schaeffer

Scott R. Burson and Jerry L. Walls, *C. S. Lewis and Francis Schaeffer* (Downers Grove: IVP, 1998).

David C. Downing, *The Most Reluctant Convert: C. S. Lewis's Journey to Faith* (Downers Grove: IVP, 2002).

Colin Duriez, *Francis Schaeffer: An Authentic Life* (Nottingham: IVP, 2008).

C. S. Lewis, *Mere Christianity* (Glasgow: Collins, 1988).

Victor Reppert, *C. S. Lewis's Dangerous Idea: In Defense of the Argument from Reason* (Downers Grove: IVP, 2003).

Francis Schaeffer, *The Complete Works of Francis Schaeffer* (Wheaton: Crossway, 1994).

The history of apologetics and philosophy

L. Russ Bush (ed.), *Classical Readings in Christian Apologetics: AD 100–1800* (Grand Rapids: Zondervan, 1983).

Kelly James Clark (ed.), *Philosophers Who Believe: The Spiritual Journeys of 11 Leading Thinkers* (Downers Grove: IVP, 1993).

Avery Dulles, *A History of Apologetics* (Eugene: Wipf & Stock, 1999).

William Edgar and K. Scott Oliphint, *Christian Apologetics Past & Present: A Primary Source Reader*, vol. 1 (Wheaton: Crossway, 2009), vol. 2 (Crossway, 2011).

Peter Hicks, *The Journey So Far: Philosophy Through the Ages* (Grand Rapids: Zondervan, 2003).

Bryan Magee, *The Story of Philosophy* (London: Dorling Kingsley, 2001).

Thomas V. Morris, *God and the Philosophers: The Reconciliation of Faith and Reason* (Oxford: OUP, 1994).

Blaise Pascal, *Pensées* (London: Penguin, 2003).

Michael Reeves, *The Breeze of the Centuries: Introducing Great Theologians – from the Apostolic Fathers to Aquinas* (Nottingham: IVP, 2010).

Contemporary culture

Peter Hitchens, *The Rage Against God* (London: Continuum, 2010).

Marcus Honeysett, *Meltdown: Making Sense of a Culture in Crisis* (Leicester: IVP, 2002).

C. S. Lewis, *The Abolition of Man* (Grand Rapids: Zondervan, 2001).

Alister McGrath, *The Twilight of Atheism* (London: Random House, 2004).

Alister McGrath, *Why God Won't Go Away: Engaging with the New Atheism* (London: SPCK, 2011).

Nancy Pearcey, *Total Truth: Liberating Christianity from Its Cultural Captivity* (Wheaton: Crossway, 2008).

James W. Sire, *The Universe Next Door* (Leicester: IVP, 1997).

The reliability of the Bible

Craig L. Blomberg, *Jesus and the Gospels* (Leicester: Apollos, 1997).

F. F. Bruce, *The New Testament Documents: Are They Reliable?* (Leicester: IVP, 1988).

Craig A. Evans, *Fabricating Jesus: How Modern Scholars Distort the Gospels* (Nottingham: IVP, 2007).

James K. Hoffmeier, *The Archaeology of the Bible* (Oxford: Lion, 2008).

James K. Hoffmeier, *Israel in Egypt* (Oxford: Oxford University Press, 1996).

Timothy P. Jones, *Misquoting Truth: A Guide to the Fallacies of Bart Ehrman's* Misquoting Jesus (Downers Grove: IVP, 2007).

Walter C. Kaiser, *The Old Testament Documents* (Leicester: IVP, 2001).

K. A. Kitchen, *On the Reliability of the Old Testament* (Grand Rapids: Eerdmans, 2003).

Lee Martin McDonald, *The Biblical Canon: Its Origin, Transmission and Authority* (Baker Academic, 2006).

Alan Millard, *Discoveries from Bible Times* (Oxford: Lion, 1997).

Amy Orr-Ewing, *Why Trust the Bible?* (Leicester: IVP, 2005).

Arthur G. Patzia, *The Making of the New Testament* (Leicester: Apollos, 1995).

The challenge of science

Paul Davies, *God and the New Physics* (London: Penguin, 1983).

William A. Dembski, *The Design Inference* (Cambridge: Cambridge University Press, 1998).

Rodney D. Holder, *God, the Multiverse, and Everything* (Aldershot: Ashgate, 2004).

Phillip E. Johnson, *Darwin on Trial*, 2nd edn (Downers Grove: IVP, 1993).

John Lennox, *God's Undertaker: Has Science Buried God?* (Oxford: Lion Hudson, 2009).

C. S. Lewis, *Miracles* (Glasgow: Collins, 1988).

Alister McGrath, *Dawkins' God* (Oxford: Blackwell, 2005).

Stephen C. Meyer, *Signature in the Cell: DNA and the Evidence for Design* (San Francisco: HarperOne, 2010).

Jay W. Richards and Guillermo Gonzalez, *The Privileged Planet: How Our Place in the Cosmos Is Designed for Discovery* (Washington DC: Regnery Publishing, 2004).

Lee Strobel, *The Case for a Creator* (Grand Rapids: Zondervan, 2004).

Jesus and the world religions

Norman Anderson, *Christianity and the World Religions* (Leicester: IVP, 1984).

Gary R. Habermas, *The Risen Jesus and Future Hope* (New York: Rowman & Littlefield, 2003).

Harold Netland, *Dissonant Voices: Religious Pluralism and the Quest for Truth* (Leicester: Apollos, 1991).

Lesslie Newbigin, *The Gospel in a Pluralist Society* (London: SPCK, 1989).

John N. Oswalt, *The Bible Among the Myths* (Grand Rapids: Zondervan, 2009).

Tom Wright, *Who Was Jesus?* (London: SPCK, 2005).

Ravi Zacharias, *Jesus Among Other Gods: The Absolute Claims of the Christian Message* (London: Thomas Nelson, 2001).

The problem of evil

D. A. Carson, *How Long, O Lord?* 2nd edn (Nottingham: IVP, 2006).

Roger Carswell, *Where Is God in a Messed-up World?* (Leicester: IVP, 2006).

Paul Copan, *Is God a Moral Monster? Making Sense of the Old Testament God* (Michigan: Baker Books, 2011).

William A. Dembski, *The End of Christianity: Finding Good in an Evil World* (Milton Keynes: Paternoster, 2009).

Paul Helm, *The Providence of God* (Leicester: IVP, 1993).
C. S. Lewis, *The Problem of Pain* (Glasgow: Collins, 2011).
N. T. Wright, *Evil and the Justice of God* (London: SPCK, 2006).

Apologetics reference texts
Apologetics Study Bible (HCSB) (Nashville: Holman Bible Publishers, 2007).
Campbell Campbell-Jack and Gavin J. McGrath (eds.), *New Dictionary of Christian Apologetics* (Leicester: IVP, 2006).
William Lane Craig and J. P. Moreland, *The Blackwell Companion to Natural Theology* (Oxford: Wiley-Blackwell, 2009).
C. Stephen Evans, *Pocket Dictionary of Apologetics and Philosophy of Religion* (Downers Grove: IVP, 2002).

Apologetics in action: books to give to a non-Christian friend
G. K. Chesterton, *Orthodoxy* (White Crow Books, 2010).
Antony Flew with Ray Abraham Varghese, *There Is a God* (San Francisco: HarperOne, 2007).
Krish Kandiah, *Destiny: What's Life All About?* (Oxford: Monarch, 2007).
Tim Keller, *The Reason for God: Belief in an Age of Scepticism* (London: Hodder & Stoughton, 2008).
Michael Ots, *What Kind of God? Responding to 10 Popular Accusations* (Nottingham: IVP, 2008).
Lee Strobel, *The Case for Faith: A Journalist Investigates the Toughest Objections to Christianity* (Grand Rapids: Zondervan, 2000).
Ravi Zacharias, *Can Man Live Without God?* (Nashville: Thomas Nelson, 1994).

Notes

1. Apology for apologetics

1. See also Acts 22:1; 24:10 and 25:8.
2. He uses the same word to describe his ministry in Philippians 1:16 and 2 Timothy 4:16–17.
3. Mark 16:8.
4. John 20:25.
5. Acts 17:32.
6. As Paul Griffiths does in *An Apology for Apologetics* (Maryknoll: Orbis, 1991), pp. 60–76.
7. James Sire, *Why Good Arguments Often Fail* (Nottingham: IVP, 2006), p. 74.
8. Ibid., pp. 78–79.
9. Jesus spoke of conversion and calling in terms of God taking the initiative (John 3:3; John 15:16; Luke 10:22). This is not to ignore a very important tension between God's sovereign work and our genuine freedom to choose. However, all steps of faith owe themselves to the sovereign work of God (such as in Ephesians 1:11).
10. Josh McDowell, *The Resurrection Factor* (Carlisle: Authentic Media, 2005).
11. Brian McLaren, *The Church on the Other Side: Exploring the Radical Future of the Local Congregation* (Grand Rapids: Zondervan, 2006), p. 171.
12. Ibid., p. 82.

2. Apologetics and philosophy

1. Colossians 2:8.
2. Many of their testimonies are found in Kelly James Clark (ed.), *Philosophers Who Believe* (Downers Grove: IVP, 1993) and Thomas V. Morris, *God and the Philosophers* (Oxford: OUP, 1994).

3. Christian persuaders

1. There have been many attempts to categorize systems of apologetics under four or five headings. This chapter will not attempt to provide that more technical discussion. For slightly different divisions, see Steven B. Cowan (ed.), *Five Views on Apologetics* (Zondervan, 2000) and Kenneth D. Boa and Robert M. Bowman (eds.), *Faith Has Its Reasons*, 2nd edn (Milton Keynes: Paternoster, 2006). In this book we are aiming to simplify the issue!
2. 1 Corinthians 2:4–5.
3. Augustine, 'On Free Will', in John Baillie, John McNeill and Henry van Dusen (eds.), *Augustine: Earlier Writings*, Library of Christian Classics, vol. 6 (Philadelphia: Westminster John Knox, 1953), p. 117.
4. Lewis Carroll, *Through the Looking Glass and What Alice Found There* (Boston: International Pocket Library, 1971), p. 86.
5. Michael Reeves, *The Breeze of the Centuries* (Nottingham: IVP, 2010), p. 108.
6. From Kierkegaard's *Journals and Papers*, cited in Boa and Bowman (eds.), *Faith Has Its Reasons*, p. 387.
7. Warfield in Boa and Bowman, *Faith Has Its Reasons*, p. 90.
8. Joseph Butler, *The Analogy of Religion*, published in 1736.
9. Habermas in Cowan (ed.), *Five Views on Apologetics*, p. 115.
10. Ibid., p. 121.
11. Josh McDowell, *The New Evidence That Demands a Verdict* (Nashville: Thomas Nelson, 1999), p. xxx of addenda.

12. Alasdair MacIntyre, *Whose Justice? Which Rationality?* (Notre Dame: University of Notre Dame Press, 1988), p. 9.
13. Nicholas Wolterstorff, *Reason Within the Bounds of Religion* (Grand Rapids: Eerdmans, 1983). The title is a deliberate play on a work by Immanuel Kant: *Religion Within the Limits of Reason Alone*. Kant put reason first and analysed the Christian faith by its light. Wolterstorff turns the argument around.
14. Wolterstorff, *Reason Within the Bounds of Religion*, p. 76.
15. Alvin Plantinga and Nicholas Wolterstorff (eds.), *Faith and Rationality: Reason and Belief in God* (London: University of Notre Dame Press, 1991), p. 90.
16. William Lane Craig, *Reasonable Faith: Christian Truth and Apologetics* (Wheaton: Crossway, 1984), p. 3.
17. Cornelius Van Til, *Christian Apologetics* (New Jersey: P. & R., 1976), p. 63.
18. See John Frame, *The Doctrine of the Knowledge of God* (New Jersey: P. & R., 1995).
19. Ibid., p. 309.
20. Van Til, *Christian Apologetics*, p. 36.

4. For the sake of argument

1. C. S. Lewis, 'Christian Apologetics', in *Compelling Reason* (Fount, 1998), p. 80.
2. Kenneth D. Boa and Robert M. Bowman, *Faith Has Its Reasons*, 2nd edn (Milton Keynes: Paternoster, 2006), p. 515.
3. The inscription is one that Paul had observed (Acts 17:23). The source of the first poetic quotation (Acts 17:28a) is unclear – it may be a paraphrase of the words of Epimenides of Crete (also cited in Titus 1:12); the second quotation (Acts 17:28b) is found in Aratus, among other Greek poets.
4. From *The God Who Is There*, in *The Complete Works of Francis Schaeffer* (Wheaton: Crossway, 1994), p. 10.

5. Colin Duriez, *Francis Schaeffer: An Authentic Life* (Nottingham: IVP, 2008), p. 174.

6. Ibid., p. 218.

7. Like most people, Lewis's conversion was a complex process. It is detailed and discussed in David C. Downing, *The Most Reluctant Convert* (Downers Grove: IVP, 2002).

8. C. S. Lewis, *Mere Christianity* (Glasgow: Collins, 1988), p. 118.

9. C. S. Lewis, *Miracles* (Glasgow: Collins, 1988), ch. 3: 'The Cardinal Difficulty of Naturalism'.

10. Lewis, *Mere Christianity*, p. 121.

11. David K. Clark, *Dialogical Apologetics* (Grand Rapids: Baker Books, 1993). Another attempt to synthesize these approaches to apologetics is made by Ronald B. Mayers, *Balanced Apologetics* (Grand Rapids: Kregel Publications, 1984).

5. Apologetics through the ages

1. Viktor E. Frankl, *The Feeling of Meaninglessness* (Milwaukee, Wisconsin: Marquette University Press, 2010), p. 220.

2. Michael Reeves, *The Breeze of the Centuries* (Nottingham: IVP, 2010), p. 76.

3. See especially Augustine, *The City of God*, Books 8–10.

4. Alvin Plantinga (ed.), *The Ontological Argument* (London: Macmillan, 1968), p. 4. The argument was given this name by later thinkers.

5. Reeves, *The Breeze of the Centuries*, p. 116.

6. Bertrand Russell, *A History of Western Philosophy* (London: Unwin, 1988), p. 175.

7. Thomas Aquinas, *Summa Contra Gentiles*, Book 2, 4:5. (London: University of Notre Dame Press, 1975), p. 35.

8. Timothy McDermott, *Summa Theologiae: A Concise Translation* (Allen, Texas: Thomas More Publishing, 1989), p. 11.

9. This is controversial, but many philosophers point out that, while infinity is a useful mathematical tool, there is no such

thing as an actual infinite. If a sequence had no beginning but stretched back into infinity, then how much time would have to pass to reach our present point in time? The answer is an infinite length of time. But, wait a moment, an infinite length of time can never pass because it is not a finite number! That means time from infinity past is never going to get to the present. This can be hard to grasp at first, but it is an important point against the idea of an actual infinite. For more explanation see William Lane Craig, *Time and Eternity: Exploring God's Relationship to Time* (Wheaton: Crossway, 2001).

10. John Calvin, *The Institutes of the Christian Religion*, trans. F. L. Battles, ed. J. T. McNeill (Westminster/SCM, 1961), 1.7.4, p. 33.

11. René Descartes, *Discourse on Method and the Meditations* (Middlesex: Penguin, 1987), p. 40.

12. Richard Tarnas, *The Passion of the Western Mind: Understanding the Ideas That Shaped Our World View* (Ballantine, 1991), p. 280.

13. John Locke, *The Reasonableness of Christianity as Delivered in the Scriptures* (London: Thoemmes Press/Routledge, 1997).

14. Immanuel Kant, *On History* (New York: Library of Liberal Arts, 1963), p. 3.

15. David Hume, *Dialogues Concerning Natural Religion* (1779) – published after his death. Second edition available, ed. Richard H. Popkin (Indiana/Cambridge: Hackett Publishing Co., 1998).

16. David Hume, *A Treatise of Human Nature*, Book 1 (1739), edited by D. G. C. Macnabb (Glasgow: Collins, 1987), p. 319.

6. Brave new world

1. A detailed discussion is provided by Nick Spencer, *Darwin and God* (London: SPCK, 2009).

2. Michael Neve and Sharon Messenger (eds.), *Autobiographies* (London: Penguin, 2002), p. 49.

3. Ibid., p. 50.

4. Ibid., p. 52.

5. Ibid., p. 53.

6. Adolf von Harnack, *What Is Christianity?* trans. Thomas Bailey Saunders (London: Ernest Been, 1958), p. 22.

7. Ibid., p. 31.

8. R. Hooykaas, *Religion and the Rise of Modern Science* (Edinburgh: Scottish Academic Press, 1984).

9. William Golding, *The Hot Gates and Other Occasional Pieces* (New York: Harcourt Brace, 1965), p. 85.

10. 'The Gay Science', section 125, in Keith Ansell Pearson and Duncan Large (eds.), *The Nietzsche Reader* (Blackwell, 2006), p. 224.

11. Ibid., p. 234.

12. 'The Anti-Christ', 18, in ibid., p. 491. Interestingly, Nietzsche spoke more favourably of Islam as a religion.

13. Douglas Rushkoff, *Children of Chaos* (London: HarperCollins, 1997), p. 269.

14. D. A. Carson, *The Gagging of God: Christianity Confronts Pluralism* (Leicester: IVP, 1996), p. 100.

15. Lesslie Newbigin, *Proper Confidence: Faith, Doubt and Certainty in Christian Discipleship* (London: SPCK, 1995), p. 27.

16. Philip D. Kenneson, 'There's No Such Thing As Objective Truth, And It's a Good Thing, Too', in Timothy R. Phillips and Dennis L. Okholm, *Christian Apologetics in the Postmodern World* (Downers Grove: IVP, 1995), p. 166.

17. Ibid., p. 169.

18. A brilliant overview of the main characters is provided by Marcus Honeysett, *Meltdown: Making Sense of a Culture in Crisis* (Leicester: IVP, 2002).

19. Jean Baudrillard, *Simulacra and Simulation* (University of Michigan, 1994).

20. Ibid., p. 79.

21. Honeysett, *Meltdown*, p. 85.

22. Jean Baudrillard, 'The Matrix Decoded: *Le Nouvel Observateur* Interview', *International Journal of Baudrillard Studies*, vol. 1:2

(July 2004) trans. Dr Gary Genosko and Adam Bryx,
Lakehead University, Ontario, Canada.

23. Robin Gill, *The 'Empty' Church Revisited* (Aldershot: Ashgate,
2003).

7. Digging up the Bible

1. See Hoffmeier, *The Archaeology of the Bible* (Oxford: Lion,
2008), pp. 11ff.

2. K. A. Kitchen, *On the Reliability of the Old Testament* (Grand
Rapids: Eerdmans, 2003) provides a comprehensive treatment
of these examples and more (pp. 313ff.).

3. Ibid., pp. 338–339.

4. A comprehensive discussion of the archaeological evidence is
provided in James K. Hoffmeier, *Israel in Egypt* (Oxford: OUP,
1996). A defence of the early date of the exodus and its
archaeological credibility is found in Walter C. Kaiser, *The Old
Testament Documents* (Leicester: IVP, 2001), pp. 109–118. A
defence of the later date of the exodus is found in K. A. Kitchen,
On the Reliability of the Old Testament, pp. 254–310.

5. Uriah is Semitic – the 'yah' ending gives away its Hebrew
roots – while the Hittites were an Indo-European people with
a language closer to Greek. This has led some scholars to
doubt that the Hittites of the Bible are the same as the
Hittites of Anatolia.

6. Kaiser, *The Old Testament Documents*, pp. 99–105.

7. T. C. Mitchell, *The Bible in the British Museum* (London: British
Museum Press, 2004), p. 52.

8. See Kaiser, *The Old Testament Documents*, pp. 45–46.

8. Science friction

1. The survey was originally conducted by James Leuba, who
wrongly predicted that belief in God would decline with the
advances of science. See Alister McGrath with Joanna

Collicutt McGrath, *The Dawkins Delusion* (London: SPCK, 2007), pp. 20–21.

2. John Calvin, *Genesis* (Edinburgh: Banner of Truth, 1965), pp. 85–86.

3. Cicero, *De Natura Deorum*, cited in Keith Thomson, *The Watch on the Heath: Science and Religion Before Darwin* (London: HarperCollins, 2005), p. 59.

4. William Paley, *Natural Theology* (Oxford: OUP, 2006), p. 7.

5. Ibid., p. 8.

6. Ibid., p. 35.

7. Michael Neve and Sharon Messenger (eds.), *Autobiographies* (London: Penguin), p. 31.

8. James Moore, *The Darwin Legend* (London: Hodder & Stoughton, 1995), p. 53.

9. Ibid., p. 47.

10. Francis Darwin (ed.), *The Life and Letters of Charles Darwin*, vol. 1 (Cambridge: CUP, 2009), p. 316.

11. See especially David N. Livingstone, *Darwin's Forgotten Defenders* (Vancouver: Regent College, 1997), pp. 112–122.

12. Nick Spencer and Denis Alexander, *Rescuing Darwin: God and Evolution in Britain Today* (London: Theos, 2009) cite a recent survey suggesting that 25% of the general population of the UK are 'ill-disposed toward Darwinian evolution' (p. 36).

13. James W. Sire, *Why Good Arguments Often Fail: Making a More Persuasive Case for Christ* (Nottingham: IVP, 2006), p. 104.

14. Richard Dawkins, *The God Delusion* (Ealing: Bantam Press, 2006), p. 79.

15. Francis Crick, *What Mad Pursuit: A Personal Journey of Scientific Discovery* (New York: Basic Books, 1990), p. 138.

16. Phillip E. Johnson, *Reason in the Balance* (Downers Grove: IVP 1995), p. 108. Phillip Johnson, a lawyer by training, has maintained a detailed critique of naturalism and evolutionary theory on the basis of its weak evidence and poor logic. See

further his introductory guide, *Testing Darwinism* (Leicester: IVP, 1997).

17. Ernst Mayr, *What Evolution Is* (London: Weidenfeld & Nicholson, 2002), p. 303.

18. Richard Dawkins, *The Greatest Show on Earth: The Evidence for Evolution* (London: Bantam Press, 2009), p. 10.

19. Ibid., p. 17.

20. Notice the diverse range of contributors to William A. Dembski's *Uncommon Dissent* (Intercollegiate Studies Institute, 2004). Books by non-Christian critics of popular Darwinism deserve particular consideration here, such as David Berlinski, *The Devil's Delusion: Atheism and Its Scientific Pretensions* (New York: Basic Books, 2009), or Jerry Fodor and Massimo Piattelli-Palmarini, *What Darwin Got Wrong* (Profile Books, 2010), which demonstrate that it is not just Christians who have a problem with Richard Dawkins!

21. David Stove, *Darwinian Fairytales: Selfish Genes, Errors of Heredity, and Other Fables of Evolution* (New York: Encounter Books, 2006), p. 325.

22. Michael Denton, *Evolution: A Theory in Crisis* (Adler & Adler, 1985). Denton is a molecular biologist and medical doctor who went on to write *Nature's Destiny: How the Laws of Biology Reveal Purpose in the Universe* (Free Press, 2002).

23. Denton, *Evolution: A Theory in Crisis*, p. 345.

24. Proposed in 1972, this theory suggests that evolution does take sudden, rapid leaps forward which are too swift to leave a record in the fossil remains. A mechanism for such rapid change is unknown, and Darwinists generally avoid this proposal.

25. Nigel Bovey, *God, the Big Bang and Bunsen-Burning Issues* (Milton Keynes: Authentic, 2008), p. 58.

26. Denton, *Evolution: A Theory in Crisis*, p. 342.

27. Francis Collins, *The Language of God: A Scientist Presents Evidence for Belief* (London: Pocket Books, 2006), p. 193.

28. Richard Dawkins, *A Devil's Chaplain* (Boston: Houghton Mifflin, 2003), p. 102.
29. Robert Jastrow, *God and the Astronomers*, 2nd edn (New York/ London: W. W. Norton & Co., 1992), p. 107.
30. David Snoke, *A Biblical Case for an Old Earth* (Grand Rapids: Baker Books, 2006), p. 128.
31. Bovey, *God, the Big Bang and Bunsen-Burning Issues*, p. 170. For much more detail see Rodney D. Holder, *God, the Multiverse, and Everything*.
32. The argument is introduced in a simple way in William Lane Craig, *On Guard: Defending Your Faith with Reason and Precision* (Eastbourne: David C. Cook, 2010), pp. 73–104. It has also been popularized by Norman Geisler.
33. Stephen Hawking and Leonard Mlodinow, *The Grand Design* (London: Bantam Press, 2010), p. 180.
34. John Lennox, *God and Stephen Hawking: Whose Design Is It Anyway?* (Oxford: Lion Hudson, 2010), p. 68.
35. Paul Davies, *God and the New Physics* (London: Penguin, 1983), p. 189.
36. C. S. Lewis, 'Christian Apologetics', in *Compelling Reason* (Fount, 1998), p. 68.
37. David Robertson, *The Dawkins Letters* (Rosshire: Christian Focus, 2007), pp. 138–139.
38. Antony Flew, in an interview with Gary Habermas, published in *Philosophia Christi* (Winter, 2005). See also Antony Flew with Ray Abraham Varghese, *There Is a God* (San Francisco: HarperOne, 2007).

9. Dealing with diversity

1. Michael Neve and Sharon Messenger (eds.), *Autobiographies* (London: Penguin), p. 52.
2. Wilfred Cantwell Smith, *What Is Scripture? A Comparative Approach* (SCM, 1993), p. 235.

3. Dan Brown, *The Da Vinci Code* (London: Bantam Press, 2004), pp. 242–243. I can count four errors in these words alone. How about you? Perhaps Brown intends for us to guess Sir Leigh Teabing is a fake? The first Dead Sea scrolls were found earlier, in 1947.

4. Paul W. Barnett, *Jesus and the Logic of History* (Leicester: Apollos, 1999), pp. 54–55.

5. Alan Millard, *Discoveries from Bible Times* (Oxford: Lion, 1997), pp. 325–326.

6. Christopher Hitchens, *God Is Not Great* (London: Atlantic Books, 2007), p. 112.

7. See J. A. T. Robinson, *Can We Trust the New Testament?* (Mowbray, 1977) and *Redating the New Testament* (Wipf & Stock, 1976), where he even gives evidence for the entire New Testament, including Revelation, being completed pre-AD 70.

8. Robinson, *Can We Trust the New Testament?* p. 86.

9. F. F. Bruce, *The New Testament Documents: Are They Reliable?* (Leicester: IVP, 1988), pp. 21ff.

10. A very helpful assessment of the way in which these non-canonical Gospels are put to use by critics of orthodox Christianity is provided by Craig A. Evans, *Fabricating Jesus* (Nottingham: IVP, 2007).

11. Ben Witherington III, *The Gospel Code: Novel Claims about Jesus, Mary Magdalene and Da Vinci* (Downers Grove: IVP, 2004), pp. 80–95.

12. Cited in Charles Sherlock, *The Doctrine of Humanity* (Leicester: IVP, 1996), p. 149.

13. N. T. Wright, *Who Was Jesus?* (London: SPCK, 1992), p. 63.

14. Generally critics will make a vague reference to the pre-Christian Egyptian Book of the Dead, but there is no reference to any of these claims in this text.

15. Craig Blomberg, 'The Credibility of Jesus' Miracles', in William A. Dembski and Michael R. Licona (eds.), *Evidence for God* (Grand Rapids: Baker Books, 2010).

16. Richard Dawkins, *The God Delusion* (Ealing: Bantam Press, 2006), p. 92.

17. Hitchens, *God Is Not Great*, p. 121.

18. Norman Anderson, *Christianity and the World Religions* (Leicester: IVP, 1984), p. 175.

10. Everybody hurts

1. Alister McGrath, *Bridge-Building: Effective Christian Apologetics* (Leicester: IVP, 1992), p. 139.

2. C. S. Lewis, *The Problem of Pain* (London: Geoffrey Bles, 1940), p. 14.

3. Greg Boyd, *Is God to Blame?* (Eastbourne: Kingsway, 2004), p. 112.

4. John Hick, *Philosophy of Religion*, 4th edn (Englewood Cliffs, New Jersey: Simon & Schuster, 1990), p. 44.

5. Ibid., p. 47.

6. Francis Schaeffer, *Genesis in Space and Time* in vol. 2 of *The Complete Works* (Wheaton: Crossway, 1994), p. 68.

7. John Milton, *Paradise Lost*, Book 12 (1674), pp. 469–478.

8. Alvin Plantinga, *God, Freedom, and Evil* (Grand Rapids: Eerdmans, 1974).

9. Paul Helm, *The Providence of God* (Leicester: IVP, 1993), p. 39.

10. Richard Dawkins, *The God Delusion* (Ealing: Bantam Press, 2006), p. 217.

11. Ibid., p. 221.

12. C. S. Lewis, *The Abolition of Man* (London: HarperCollins / Fount, 1978), p. 23.